Catechesis

Catechesis

Sermons for the Christian Year

Andrew C. Mead

Foreword by Jon Meacham

Saint Thomas Church Fifth Avenue
New York

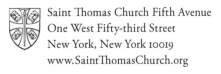 Saint Thomas Church Fifth Avenue
One West Fifty-third Street
New York, New York 10019
www.SaintThomasChurch.org

Andrew Craig Mead was ordained an Episcopal priest
in 1971 and was an assistant parish priest in England,
Connecticut and Boston. From 1978 he was a parish
rector—in Rosemont, Pennsylvania, for seven years; in
Boston for eleven years; and from 1996 to 2014, when he
retired, at Saint Thomas Church Fifth Avenue in New
York City. After a public school education, he received
his B.A. from DePauw University in Indiana, his B.D.
(M.Div.) from Yale University Divinity School, and his
M.Litt. from Oxford University in England. He and his
wife, Nancy, have a daughter, Emma; a son, Matthew,
who is also an Episcopal priest and rector; and four
grandchildren.

Cover photos © H. S. Cross 2014

First edition 2014
ISBN: 9780-9903020-0-1
Library of Congress Control Number: 2014937754

Contents

Foreword

*We preach not ourselves, but Christ Jesus as Lord; and
ourselves your servants for Jesus' sake.* —2 Corinthians 4:5

As a rule, clergymen like the sound of their own voices. Little
wonder: From the beginning of their sacramental lives, priests
are imbued with a sense of their indispensability to the life of the
Church and to the cause of Christ. In the ordination rite of the 1928
Book of Common Prayer, the bishop reminds those about to enter
the priesthood about "how high a Dignity, and to how weighty an
Office and Charge ye are called: that is to say, to be Messengers,
Watchmen, and Stewards of the Lord; to teach, and to premonish, to
feed and provide for the Lord's family; to seek for Christ's sheep that
are dispersed abroad, and for his children who are in the midst of
this naughty world, that they may be saved through Christ for ever."

When Andrew Mead heard those words more than four
decades ago, he was, as he often says, ready to "hop to it" for the
sake of the one holy catholic and apostolic faith. Nineteen seventy-
one, a year in which the upheavals of the 1960s were spreading, not
receding, was not perhaps the most likely of moments for a young
man to embrace the old over the new, the traditional over the novel,
the canonical over the revolutionary. Yet the young Andrew understood then what the older Andrew has practiced ever since: that the
message and mission of the crucified and risen Lord Jesus is in fact
the most radical story in human history—a story at once so funda-
mental and overwhelming that it requires no embroidery and little

elaboration. The core is sufficient, for the core is Christ, and Christ is everything.

And so it is that Father Mead, who is in 2014 ending his tenure as Rector and Priest of Saint Thomas Church Fifth Avenue, is that most unlikely of clergymen. He preaches pithily, happy to make his point and then get on with things—to hop to it. Yes, he has been a Messenger, a Watchman, and a Steward of the Lord's, but he has done so with a minimum of ego and a persistent, successful resistance to creating a cult of personality. He is not the main thing. Jesus is.

Taken together, the sermons collected here record a priestly life spent in pursuit of the simplest yet most profound truths of Christianity. In three ways this volume underscores Father Mead's insistence on returning again and again, in times of war and of peace, of plenty and of want, to the proper answer to the question Jesus once put to his disciples: "Who do men say that I am?"

First, unlike most sermons in this or any age, they are brief. Not superficial, mind you, but clear and to the point. "To preach more than half an hour," said the English evangelist George Whitefield, "a man should be an angel himself or have angels for hearers." Andrew—however much we love him—is no angel, and I can safely say that his congregation (at least when I am there) is not universally angelic. Thus the eight to ten minutes or so that the Rector claims of sacred time in the midst of the Holy Eucharist is just exactly right.

Second, Andrew has managed a most difficult task from the pulpit: He has kept his eyes—and thus the ears of his hearers—on the great truths of the faith, struggling mightily to keep the theological and ecclesiastical battles of the moment at bay. The Homer of Anglicanism, Anthony Trollope, once observed: "The apostle of Christianity and the infidel can meet without a chance of a quarrel; but it is never safe to bring together two men who differ about a saint or a surplice." The same goes for the politics of the secular arena. Andrew's view—and it is an uncommon one—is that there is world enough and time for the disputes and debates inherent to life. The pulpit and the altar should be in the world but not of it. Those of us who make our way in from the hurly burly of Fifth Avenue tend to come for things eternal, not things temporal. And the sermons in this book reflect a Rector's determination to speak to the times of the truth of all times. Headlines come and go. The Cross is forever.

Which brings us to the third person of this particular trinity of homiletic virtues: the deep and abiding commitment to focusing our attention not on ourselves but on the crisis at Calvary. The priesthood is partly a theatrical office. The task of the ordained is to recreate and reenact—and above all to remember, in obedience to the Lord's commandment in the Upper Room. Theatrical people, not uncommonly, like attention, and they understandably seek affection and applause. That requires conducting yourself in such a manner that all available eyes fall on you; all hearts rise and fall with you; all hope is fixed on you. Yet the reader of these sermons will soon appreciate what those of us who were fortunate enough to hear many of them know from experience: that more often than not, at a critical passage in a sermon, Andrew Mead would draw attention not to himself but to one of two places in the great nave of Saint Thomas, either to the Crucifix on the pillar to the preacher's left in the pulpit or to the altar over his right shoulder. Those with eyes to see and ears to hear therefore know that the messenger is not the most important thing—the message itself is.

That message is, at heart, the message of the Gospels and the creeds. C. S. Lewis, another Anglo-Catholic, would have approved of Andrew's sermons. "The great difficulty is to get modern audiences to realize that you are preaching Christianity solely and simply because you happen to think it true; they always suppose you are preaching it because you like it or think it good for society or something of that sort," Lewis wrote in *Mere Christianity*, his wartime defense of the faith. "Now a clearly maintained distinction between what the Faith actually says and what you would like it to have said or what you understand or what you personally find helpful or think probable, forces your audience to realize that you are tied to your data just as the scientist is tied by the results of the experiments; that you are not just saying what you like."

There we have it—and in this book you have the collected sermons of a good man, a good priest and a good friend. On that day in 1971 when Andrew was ordained, he heard these words: "See that ye never cease your labour, your care and diligence, until ye have done all that lieth in you, according to your bounden duty, to bring all such as are or shall be committed to your charge, unto that agreement in the faith and knowledge of God, and to that ripeness and perfectness of age in Christ, that there be no place left among you, either for error in religion, or for viciousness in life." Few priests can have so conscientiously fulfilled that sacred charge as Andrew Mead has. Those of us who have known him and loved him owe him the greatest of debts.

Jon Meacham

2014

Preface

I am at heart a catechist, a teacher of the faith. I find myself catechizing, directly or indirectly, no matter what I am doing in parish ministry, even at Vestry Meetings. More to the heart of things, I find as a pastor, in "the care of souls" with individuals, my most effective means of grace is the straightforward but gentle presentation of the Gospel, the faith of Christ, put forward directly into the crux of whatever the pastoral concern is. Pastoral catechizing shows up broadly, week after week, in sermons within the liturgy.

Leaders of communities must engage in repetition in order to get the basic messages across. This maxim holds even more for leaders of churches. There is little need—far from it—for a good preacher to seek to be innovative or original in content. Descriptions such as "novel" or "unheard of" are among the adjectives for heresy, whereas "apostolic" and "catholic" mean that faith that has been sent from the beginning and believed everywhere, always, by all. In the Apostle's phrase, priests receive from the Lord that which we deliver to you—whether it be the Word or the Sacraments. However, the need for faithful repetition makes the preacher's task more challenging, because the same message must continually be reclothed to fit life as it grows and develops. In addition, the preacher must dig deeply into the unsearchable riches of Christ and then make them accessible to the hearers. When I look back to see what I have preached in the past on a given text (the Episcopal Church has a three-year rotation of Sunday Scriptures), I find that I cannot reuse an old sermon, even when I mean to convey the same substance. Circumstances, the congregation and I have developed over three years. The perennial message must be recast.

One of my favorite jobs since I first became a rector of a parish in 1978 has been my Rector's Christian Doctrine Class, which consists of fourteen or more sessions and covers the range of the Church Catechism from Creation and Fall to the Last Judgment. My weekly sermons, as they follow the cycle of the Christian Year, observe a similar pattern. The sermons in this volume, gathered as I prepare to retire as Rector of Saint Thomas, span a period of my eighteen years serving this amazing church. Some are stories, some are biblical exposition, and some are church doctrine. They average 900 to 1,200 words each—about nine to twelve minutes. I have increasingly come to prefer shorter preachments, to believe that less is more, and that often the best way to finish a sermon is simply to stop. Most of these sermons were within the Eucharist on Sunday morning. A few were at Evensong—which allows more leeway. A few were occasional and preached as a guest elsewhere. All, I trust, set forth the Gospel of Jesus, most supremely Christ Crucified.

Clergy are ordained to deliver the Gospel and the catholic, apostolic faith of the Church. In my years as a priest since 1971 three general abuses of the pulpits in churches by clergy have come in successive waves: (1) using the sermon to advance a political agenda; (2) using the sermon to engage in psycho-babble; and, more recently, (3) using the sermon to focus on the person of the preacher. Of course the Gospel often touches upon politics, or psychology, or the personal life of the homilist, and these can be useful introductions to the Gospel. But the subject is the Good News of Jesus. The Apostle has it, as ever, just right: "We preach not ourselves, but Christ Jesus as Lord; and ourselves your servants for Jesus' sake" (2 Cor. 4:5). It is my hope that my teaching and preaching over two decades at Saint Thomas has revolved, with the Christian Year, around the lifesaving mystery who is Jesus Christ our Lord and God, and that Christ's Gospel has been duly heard and received.

Thanks first and last to Heather Cross for editorial oversight and organization, and for the photography and design of the cover. An acute listener to sermons herself, she has made all the difference. Thanks to Victor Austin, whose books I admire and who showed by example and counsel how a book is done. Thanks to Jon Meacham, who arrived at Saint Thomas when I did and has been, as his Foreword to these sermons reveals, a hearer, a counselor and a friend all along. Thanks to Charlotte Wiggers for her astute, meticulous copyediting and proofreading. Thanks to David Daniel and Douglas Robbe for retrieval of sermons from the sermon archives and files; David's work over the years with the archiving of sermons on the website has been masterful. I thank Francis Blouin for the start of this project as a matter for the Saint Thomas archives, and I thank as well the several parishioners who over the years have asked for such a published collection. Thanks to our Church Wardens, William Wright and Kenneth Koen, for their support and suggestions. Most of all, thanks to the people of Saint Thomas, so eager to hear and receive God's holy Word, who have by their hearing shaped for the better every sermon I have delivered. They are in some sense coauthors with me. To them and to Nancy Mead, the most supportive and critical hearer of them all, this book is dedicated.

Andrew C. Mead

2014

The Mystery of Goodness

THE LESSONS FROM HOLY SCRIPTURE that were read this morning[1] are the ones appointed by the Church's Book of Common Prayer for this Sunday in September. They are all on the theme of God's mercy, culminating with Jesus' parables of the Lost Sheep and the Lost Coin. It is important to know and remember that God is, above all, loving and merciful. But this is a unique time with special demands. My other "text" is what has been happening since last Tuesday, September 11.

The question everyone is constantly asking is, Why, how, can God allow this to happen? I have struggled with this question in other grievous situations over the thirty years of my ministry in the Church. It is the same question posed by the Book of Job. Billy Graham posed it on Friday at the National Cathedral. The answer is, I don't know. It is a mystery. Evil is a deep mystery, going all the way back to the devil and his own rebellion against the Creator. Jesus has taught us that God is both almighty and good; why God permits evil of this kind is a mystery. And as we know from the horrible

---

1 September 16, 2001: Luke 15:1–10, 1 Tim. 1:12–17, Exod. 32:1, 12–17.

scene a few miles downtown, evil can be destructive and malicious beyond our capacity to imagine.

On the other hand, no one asks, Why does good happen? Do you know, that is a deep mystery too. Goodness is a mystery. That is what I am going to speak about this morning: the mystery of goodness.

Jesus Christ taught us, among other things, that God is almighty and good, his almighty and good Father and ours as well, if we follow Jesus' lead. The very existence of the world is God's act of goodwill: "Let there be light." And the salvation of the world through Christ is God's act of love. Christ came that we might have eternal life.

All week our attention has been focused on death and dying. The victims at the World Trade Center, at the Pentagon and in the hijacked airplanes did not get up last Tuesday expecting to die. They all got up thinking they had time to work on or finish all sorts of plans, projects and relationships. Don't we all!

God, who is indeed almighty and good, will take care of those victims. The ones who died are in the arms of his mercy. They are delivered from the burden of the flesh. Their souls are in the Lord's good hands.

And God will bless the injured, and the families and friends of the victims. If they are willing, if they ask him, they will discover God's grace and mercy even in their pain.

God will also bless our country, and the many good nations that will join us to fight the great wickedness that has assaulted America and the rest of the free world, to defeat terrorism. We will have to be courageous and resolute in this war. And we must pray that our "quiet, unyielding anger" (to quote the President's speech) is purified and prevented from turning into the same kind of ungodly rage (at home and abroad) that has been visited upon us. That would be a great defeat, God forbid; it would be a victory for the Evil One himself.

But let's talk a little more about the dying and the mystery of goodness. First of all, let's understand something. This morning, when you got up and looked in the mirror, you saw one of the dying. We all know this, but in order to function "normally" we push this thought out of our minds. Yet we all know, and should not try to deny or forget, that not one of us is going to get out of this world alive. Each of us has an appointment with death.

The victims at the World Trade Center, at the Pentagon and in the hijacked airplanes had this appointment, which we all realize but do not often seriously entertain—they had this appointment thrust in their faces Tuesday morning. They knew they had only a very little time left, a few minutes. What some of those victims did with those minutes provides us with a priceless gift, a lesson from the dying on how to live, a lesson about the mystery of goodness.

There was the man on the plane that crashed in rural Pennsylvania instead of God knows where the hijackers intended. He called his family to say he and his fellow passengers knew they were doomed; they knew what the hijackers were up to, but they were "going to do something about this." It appears that they did take action that may well have averted yet another catastrophe.

Then there were the people in the Twin Towers, the ones who knew they could not escape from the inferno caused by the exploding planes that hit the buildings. They called their families and loved ones to tell them they loved them. In the midst of all that hell, those magic, mysterious words were spoken: "I love you."

Then there are the firefighters and the police, so many of whom lost their lives because, in the words of the hymn "America the Beautiful," they "loved mercy more than life." They are joined by the living: their comrades and the soldiers and the rescue and medical workers, counselors, clergy of all sorts, volunteers of every kind. And behind them countless people who want to do something to help. This is an overwhelming multitude, a great body of compassion and love, a mighty army of goodwill and prayer.

On Friday, we were caught flat-footed at our noon Eucharist. We had expected perhaps a few hundred people at that Mass. After all, the President had asked us to pray. But instead of a few hundred, we had standing room only, probably two thousand. We were caught by surprise, but the Lord provided wonderfully. It was very moving. Similar scenes occurred in many places.

This great army of goodwill is not only in the city but also in the nation and around the world. Here at Saint Thomas alone, we have been inundated by messages of love and offers to help, not just from New York and the rest of the United States, but from North India to Uruguay, to England and Ireland, to Germany and Japan. This is the great mystery of goodness, and it connects us to the almighty and good God, the Father of our Lord Jesus Christ.

If you think your little acts of goodness do not count, you are mistaken. Think again. Think of those good, brave victims on the planes and in the buildings. Think of the police and firefighters. Think of the nurses and doctors. Think of the great multitude, that mighty army of goodwill they represent. You and I have been called to be soldiers in that army.

We have already said that God created the world out of goodwill and that he has saved his world by Christ out of love. There is one more thing. The mystery of goodness has the first word, but it also has the last word. God will judge the world, including us, by the standard of goodness. What did Jesus say? He said that the King will draw up all the nations before him at the End, to judge them for all eternity. And the difference between the sheep and the goats consists of the "little" acts of goodness. The Lord is very clear and precise—"I was hungry, thirsty, sick, in prison, naked, dying, suffering, and you ministered to me. And inasmuch as you did this to the least, you did it to me."

So, my brothers and sisters, let us remember to do goodness. Let us never forget the two sentences said by the people who knew they were dying, who had only a few more minutes to live. "We're going to do something about this" and "I love you." This is the mystery of goodness. Time is short and precious, eternity is long. The things we do really matter. If we embrace goodness, if we, like the firefighters, "love mercy more than life," we will not die. We will have life forever, life in the almighty, good God.

Prayer for the Dead

L AST SUNDAY, THE FIRST SUNDAY IN NOVEMBER, we celebrated All Saints, a great festival that honors the triumphs of Christ in his most faithful servants. We have made it our custom on November's second Sunday, which is always near Veterans Day, to observe Remembrance Sunday. This custom began in England after the First World War, when the overwhelming numbers of the dead drove the nation to its knees. Since then there have been other wars, notably the Second World War, when the survival of the entire Free World was at stake as many millions more were killed.

But there is much more to remember. Here at Saint Thomas we include our congregation's departed brethren, kinsfolk and benefactors who have passed along to us this goodly heritage. And now for the past decade we have included the victims of the 9/11 terrorist attacks.

The Church Calendar provided well for this remembrance long ago, when it appointed All Souls Day following directly upon All Saints—that is, November first and then second—as a day of prayer for all the faithful departed that, in the words of one of the prayers, in the day of Christ's appearing "they may be manifested as thy children."

If the saints are the holy ones in heaven, then what about all the other souls of the faithful, and those beyond the visible community of faith? There is no compromise to be made with holiness. It calls for us as our God-given destiny, and we turned toward it when we first were attracted to Jesus. Each of us, as we decide to respond to Christ, is on the way. It is a journey headed only one way—toward and ever more deeply into the kingdom of heaven. There is no turning back. Well, there is, but consider what that means. Every aspect of our life is subject to this call and to this pilgrimage.

Holiness, for us, means at last becoming that person whom God our Father truly created us to be; for whom God in Christ went to the cross to save from sin; whom God the Holy Spirit blessed with the faith and the will to follow Christ. It is a life's work of grace. In our hearts we know this work is unfinished business. I remember a sign in the office of a parish priest: "Be patient. God isn't finished with me yet." That is the truth, and the saints themselves, more acutely than the rest of us regulars, knew this truth about themselves in their own hearts.

When we pray for the dead we remember them and hold them in our love and gratitude. But we may do more than that. We pray *for* them. What for? We pray for God to finish and perfect the good work that he began in them—to bring it to completion, to fruition in fullness. Some of our great prayers from The Book of Common Prayer express this well:

At the time of death: "Depart O Christian soul out of this world, in the name of God the Father Almighty who created you; in the Name of Jesus Christ who redeemed you; in the Name of the

Holy Spirit who sanctifies you. May your rest be this day in peace, and your dwelling place in the paradise of God."[1]

At the arrival of the body at the Church for the funeral: "Deliver your servant, O Sovereign Lord Christ, from all evil, and set him free from every bond; that he rest with all your saints in the eternal habitations."[2]

At the end of the funeral, by the coffin: "Acknowledge, we humbly beseech thee, a sheep of thine own fold, a lamb of thine own flock, a sinner of thine own redeeming. Receive her into the arms of thy mercy, into the blessed rest of everlasting peace, and into the glorious company of the saints in light."[3]

And there are many more such prayers, all of which ask that, by virtue of the life-giving sacrifice of Jesus Christ, all souls may be washed in the Blood of the sinless Lamb of God, purged and cleansed from every stain of sin, and presented pure and spotless before God, ready to rise in resurrection splendor.[4] It's a lot to pray for.

I have long felt that the Requiem Mass, the celebration of the Sacrament of Christ's Death and Resurrection and his Real Presence in his Body and Blood on behalf of the souls departed this life, is among the most powerful and comforting of all the rites of the Church.

And it is a great comfort. It is a comfort beyond words to know we are not to be as people without hope concerning those who have died. The souls of the righteous are indeed in the hand of God where

---

1 The Book of Common Prayer (1979), p. 464.

2 *Ibid.*, p. 466.

3 *Ibid.*, p. 483.

4 *Ibid.*, p. 488.

no torment will touch them. They are in peace, the peace of Jesus Christ. This peace is grounded on the glory of Easter. For if we believe that Jesus died and rose again, then Jesus is more than able to wake them from sleep, to claim them for his own, and to bestow on them the glory of his resurrection. Rest eternal grant unto them, O Lord, and let light perpetual shine upon them.

Let God Be God

THE LITTLE BOOK OF JONAH may be the best known of all the prophets in Holy Scripture. Great as Isaiah and Jeremiah are, their narratives are not so familiar as is Jonah's being cast overboard and then saved by being swallowed by a great fish, which after three days vomited him up on the shore.

Why was Jonah cast overboard? Because he was running away from a commission given him by the Lord. When a great storm, hurled by the Lord, threatened the ship, the mariners tried everything: calling on their own gods, throwing the cargo overboard, and finally casting lots on one another to see who might be to blame. The lot fell on Jonah, and when the mariners discovered he was a Hebrew fleeing from the presence of his God, Jonah advised them to throw him into the sea. The sea calmed. Then came the great fish, or, as the story traditionally goes, the whale.

Why was Jonah running away? He went in exactly the opposite direction the Lord told him to go. Jonah took to sea; the Lord had called Jonah to go to Nineveh, the great city at the center of Assyria, ancient Israel's mightiest, most feared and hated enemy. There the Lord said the prophet was to "cry against their wickedness; for their wickedness has come up before me." Was Jonah afraid? Undoubtedly, but there was more, and this comes out in today's reading, which is the end of the story, the crucial part, and not as well known as the part about Jonah and the whale.

Vomited back onto dry land, Jonah went to Nineveh and took the word of the Lord a day's journey into the great city, crying: "Yet forty days, and Nineveh shall be overthrown." Amazingly, the people believed and the king ordered everyone, man and beast alike, to put on sackcloth, to fast, and to "turn everyone from his evil way and from the violence which is in his hands. Who knows, God may yet repent and turn from his fierce anger, so that we do not perish." Sure enough, when God saw Nineveh's repentance, God repented on his part from the evil he said he would do to them.

This turnabout angered Jonah, and he appears to have feared it from the outset. "Is this not, Lord, what I said...now take my life and let me die." "Do you do well to be angry?" said the Lord. Jonah waited and waited to see what God would do; nothing. He made himself comfortable in his wait. God appointed a bush to grow up to shade him, which made him glad. But then God had a worm destroy the bush and caused the hot sun and sultry wind to oppress Jonah, who again said he was fed up, angry enough to die. God has the last word. "You are angry, concerned about the bush which came and went in a night. Well, do I not have a right to be concerned about Nineveh, that great city, with 120,000 people who don't know their right hand from the left, and also many animals?"

Jesus liked this story and refers to it. There seem to be good reasons. Jonah, like Jesus, was from Galilee. Jonah's three-day adventure with the whale in "the belly of hell" may be likened to Christ's three-day journey from death to resurrection. And God's message through Jonah, no matter how reluctantly delivered by the prophet, is of universal mercy to those who turn from death to life.

Before we smile at Jonah's rebellion and anger, we might look at this last issue—the message he delivered and those to whom he delivered it—more closely. Do we really want our enemies to receive mercy? The Assyrians were known for their infamous brutality to those many nations they conquered. We could go to the Middle East, right to the lands of ancient Israel and Assyria, and see the problem this very day. Some enemies do horrible things. Let's bring the problem closer. In the sphere of personal and domestic life, many cruel things happen. Animosity runs deep. Many times in my ministry people have come with problems over forgiving, let alone loving, their enemies, as Christ teaches. Some things, it seems, are unforgivable.

A priest I knew who was headmaster of a ranch that was a venerable home and school for abused children once told a story of a graduate of his school, a woman, who came back to him with severe depression; she sought his counsel. Her father had violently abused her and her brother when they were little. The father had gone to prison and had died. The woman had gone on to some measure of adult success but was dogged by depression, which she knew focused on her father. She had lived in spite of him. She could not forgive him. The priest said he completely sympathized with her feelings. But could she let go of her father, give him over to God? Could she give God her permission, if he so chose, to forgive him? Could she let God be God? She had not considered giving over the whole business of her father's destiny to God. And what if it included God's mercy in some way? Well, it's a bit like Jonah and Nineveh. The conversation didn't work like magic, but it was a turning point for the woman. She let her father go. Without telling God what to do, she let God mind her father's business. Her depression began to lift. She had been angry, angry enough to die. Now she began to live some more.

The story of Jonah and the whale is no more fantastic than the fact that the Book of Jonah was written at all and included in the Hebrew canon of the prophets of Holy Scripture. Put it alongside the Book of Nahum, a diatribe of judgment against Nineveh; Jonah is a breathtaking story of mercy to the same people. But in order for the story to take hold, then or now, we have to stop being angry, sometimes angry enough to die, and let God be God. For as the prophet said in his complaint: "O Lord, is this not what I said when while I was still in my own country...for I knew that you are a gracious God and merciful, slow to anger, and abounding in steadfast love, and ready to relent from punishing." Perhaps in time we can even allow this mercy to touch us, so that even our deepest feelings begin to be healed by this very same God.[1]

---

1 Preached at Canterbury Cathedral, September 18, 2011, at Choral Eucharist.

Saint Puddleglum

[Thomas] said to them, "Unless I see in his hands the print of the nails, and place my finger in the mark of the nails, and place my hand in his side, I will not believe." —John 20:24–31

C. S. LEWIS'S THE CHRONICLES OF NARNIA is the classic seven-book epic of the pilgrimage of a family of four schoolchildren, two brothers and two sisters, through magical lands and enchanted adventures. There are tests of soul and struggles of good against evil. There is one character in particular, a lion named Aslan, who suffers and dies and rises again, and who leads the children through great perils and to amazing victories over a great serpent who takes the beguiling form of a seductive and cruel witch. There is even a great Last Battle, which ends with the children entering and reigning with Aslan in his Kingdom.

In the middle of this epic there appears one striking little creature named Puddleglum. Puddleglum is a marsh-wiggle. He lives in a great flat plain cut by countless channels of water into little low islands covered with coarse grass and bordered by reeds and rushes. He has green–gray hair, dark skin with a muddy complexion, webbed feet and sunken cheeks. He wears a perpetually solemn expression on his long, thin and tight-lipped face. Even the smoke from Puddleglum's pipe trickles out of the bowl and downward, drifting along the ground like a mist.

Puddleglum is one of the heroes of Lewis's great story, first impressions notwithstanding. He has a pessimistic yet winning turn of mind, with expressions such as these: "Good morning. I don't mean it won't turn to rain or fog or even snow and thunder." Or "I see you're making the best of a bad job. You've been well brought up, you have. Learned to put a good face on things." Or "Puddleglum's my name. It doesn't matter if you forget it; I can always tell you again."

But Puddleglum is a staunch friend, the kind of person you want next to you in a fight. Quietly deciding to help the children on their journey, he says: "I don't know that anyone can exactly *help*... What with enemies, and mountains and rivers to cross, and losing our way, and next to nothing to eat, and sore feet, at least we'll hardly notice the [bad] weather... So don't lose heart." When he goes into a terrifying battle, he says: "Well, the cause is probably lost, but we might as well make a good end of it."[1]

My brothers and sisters in Christ, meet Saint Thomas the Apostle, the patron saint of our beloved church!

Saint Thomas is on the reredos and the facade of this church, just over the door behind his great statue, where his life is spelled out in small panels. They are called the Despair of Saint Thomas, the

---

1   C. S. Lewis, *The Silver Chair* (New York: Collier Books, 1976), 54–66.

Doubt of Saint Thomas, the Confession of Saint Thomas and the Mission of Saint Thomas. Let's look at each of these briefly.

The Despair of Saint Thomas comes in two episodes in Saint John's Gospel. The first is when Jesus, against the advice of his friends, decides to return to Judea (where his enemies are concentrated) to visit Bethany—to visit the sisters Mary and Martha and their brother Lazarus (whom he will raise from the dead). Everyone is frightened. Then Thomas says, "Let us go, that we may die with him" (John 11:16). You can read these words on the Narthex floor at the entrance to the Chantry Chapel and in the Chancel: "Let us go, that we may die with him."

Later, when gloom gathers around Jesus in his approaching passion, the Lord tells the apostles, "I go to prepare a place for you, and you know the way where I am going." Thomas says what everyone is thinking but is afraid to say: "Lord, we do not know where you are going; how can we know the way?" To which Jesus replies, "I am the way" (John 14:1–6).

The Despair of Thomas nevertheless contains honorable pluck, and by this time it doesn't surprise that, after Jesus' death, when Thomas misses his resurrection appearance to the apostles in the Upper Room on the first Easter evening, he says this as he is told by the others that they have seen the risen Lord: "Unless I see in his hands the print of the nails, and place my finger in the mark of the nails, and place my hand in his side, I will not believe." Thus the Doubt of Saint Thomas proceeds from the secret strengths of his character, revealed in the Despair of Saint Thomas. He loves the Lord. He doesn't want to hear stories of spirits or of causes outliving their founder. He doesn't want "spin." He wants to see Jesus, Jesus who was crucified.

The virtues of Thomas's Doubt are manifested on the first Sunday after Easter in the same Upper Room, as we heard in today's Gospel. The doors were locked, and Jesus appeared in their midst, meeting Thomas on his own ground. "Put your finger here, and see my hands; and put out your hand and place it in my side; do not be faithless but believing."

The Gospel doesn't say whether Thomas did touch Jesus. But Thomas obeyed Jesus by being faithful, and he made the highest confession of faith of all the apostles: "My Lord and my God." You can see him doing this, in the tableau just over the altar, kneeling before Jesus.

The Mission of Saint Thomas, according to tradition, took him east, all the way to Persia and India, where ancient churches still claim him as their founder. This remarkable character was surely a prince among the apostles, a great soldier for Christ. His mission goes on. It is here with us, and I want to finish by describing that mission.

Notice that it was *the wounds of the Body of the risen Christ* that convinced Saint Thomas and inspired his great confession of faith. That still holds true. Jesus told Thomas that those of us who have not seen with our eyes the glorious scars on the resurrected Lord are blessed through him: "Blessed are those who have not seen and yet have believed." Yet Thomas nailed down a principle by which many of us come to believe that Jesus lives. This is how it happens:

The members of the Body of Christ who most convince me that Jesus lives are the true saints. These are the Christians who really do take up their crosses daily and follow him. They bear in their own lives the living sacrifice of Jesus. In their honesty, their kindness, their courage, their generosity, their self-forgetful humility, their divine sense of humor, they show the print of the nails and the mark of the spear wound. They live by Christ, and they show that he lives and reigns in them. Their triumphs are Christ's triumphs in them. They constitute the authentic Church, the genuine Body of the same Christ who suffered for us and our salvation, died and rose again.

The Mission of Saint Thomas is for us to *be that kind of a Church; to be a family of those sorts of Christians.* This great parish, named after this extraordinary apostle—this wonderful "Puddleglum" character—has a mission to show forth Christ crucified and risen in the middle of New York.

Saint Barnabas, Son of Encouragement

He was a good man, and full of the Holy Ghost, and
of faith; and much people was added unto the Lord.
—Acts of the Apostles 11:19–30

IT IS AN ANCIENT TRADITION of the Church during Eastertide to read from Saint Luke's Book of the Acts of the Apostles. Acts shows the life of the apostolic Church in the wake of Jesus' death and resurrection. The book could be titled the Acts of the Holy Spirit, for it reveals the transformation brought about in the formerly meek and perplexed followers of Jesus, changed into the bold witnesses of the risen Lord—into the movement that turned the world upside down.

For the most part, Saints Peter and Paul are the stars of Acts. A brief, shining moment goes to Saint Stephen, the first martyr for the Name of Jesus Christ. But in today's reading we see another figure of immense importance who worked behind the public scenes, Saint Barnabas. He receives in today's reading an extraordinary encomium from Luke: "He was a good man, and full of the Holy Ghost, and of faith." It is time we learned about this apostle and martyr, for whom

The Book of Common Prayer has always devoted a major feast day on June 11, and whose life and example are of relevance to us at Saint Thomas Church.

Today's reading from Acts is not Luke's first mention of Barnabas, but it is a good place to begin. After the stoning of Stephen, the disciples of Jesus scattered for safety from the dangerous environs of Jerusalem. That was how some got to Antioch on the Orontes River in what is now Lebanon. These dispersed disciples then preached Jesus not only to their fellow Jews but to Greeks, Gentiles. So the Church at Antioch was from the start a mixture of Jewish and Gentile followers of Christ who were, at Antioch, called Christians for the first time. This new church attracted a "great number," and the Jerusalem leaders dispatched Barnabas to report on Antioch. Why Barnabas?

His real name was Joseph. Barnabas is a nickname given him by the apostles. Jesus had nicknamed some of them (Simon he called Peter; James and John he called "sons of thunder," for instance). They called Joseph "Bar-Nabas," which meant "son of encouragement" or "son of consolation." He was a "Comforter," a "Strengthener," words close to Christ's name for the Holy Spirit, the Paraclete. He was a Levite, of a wealthy Jewish family, born in Cyprus, cousin of Saint Mark the Evangelist, related to Mark's mother—the woman who provided Jesus and the apostles with the Upper Room in Jerusalem. Some early church fathers[1] say Barnabas was among the seventy whom the Lord sent out in addition to the first twelve apostles; in any case, Barnabas was called an apostle. He won his nickname by making a very large donation to the early church, apparently its

---

1   Clement of Alexandria and Eusebius the historian.

first capital gift, in the form of proceeds from the sale of real estate, money he laid at the apostles' feet. The grateful apostles gave him his nickname then—the "son of encouragement" (Acts 4:32–37).

After the martyrdom of Stephen and after the amazing conversion of his persecutor Saul into the Apostle Paul, Barnabas broke the ice between Paul and the Jerusalem leadership (who were afraid of him), joining their hands and establishing communication and trust (Acts 9:27). Barnabas had the stature and credibility, and the goodwill and faith, to do it. This was one of the most momentous connections made in history.

So Barnabas, in today's reading from Acts, once he sees the grace of God at work in the new Jewish–Gentile Christian fellowship at Antioch, rejoices and summons Paul from his home in Tarsus; and the two together help build up the new church. After a time, when famine strikes the Holy Land, the grateful Antioch church sends help to the Jerusalem church by the hands of Barnabas and Paul, which is where our reading today ends.

There is more to Barnabas's story worth heeding. Barnabas and Paul later left Antioch again to go on what is known as Paul's first missionary journey (Acts 13:3). They took with them Barnabas's young cousin Mark, sailed to Barnabas's native Cyprus, and from there to Asia Minor (modern Turkey), where they made a circuit of cities and established churches best known in the New Testament from Paul's notable Epistle to the Galatians. However, early in this journey Mark deserted Barnabas and Paul and returned home. When a second missionary journey was undertaken, Barnabas wanted Mark to have a second chance to accompany them. Paul wouldn't have it; he and Barnabas sharply disagreed, and they went separate ways, Barnabas taking Mark with him (Acts 15:36ff.). The good news is that later Mark was reconciled to Paul and was of service to him—this was probably after Barnabas's death (Col. 4:10).

We hear no more of Barnabas in Acts. Paul, who in his letters refers to him with fondness and esteem, once criticized Barnabas for not standing up to Peter in a controversy, yet even there Paul speaks with respect. The tradition is that Barnabas was martyred in his native Cyprus. His stature was secure as a man of goodness, a leader full of the Holy Spirit and of faith, and he is spoken of in Scripture as an evident saint. He embodied what our Lord commands repeatedly in today's Gospel: that we love one another as he has loved us, even to the laying down of our life.

Saint Barnabas is a character who resonates and inspires here at Saint Thomas. Well-to-do but sacrificially generous to the church, he was a man of peace and reconciliation, of faith and boldness in making connections for God's Kingdom. He was traditional and conservative in belief yet liberal and generous toward others amidst the growing pains that tried the early church. He must have been impressive to behold: When he and Paul healed a cripple on their Galatian mission, the amazed pagans tried to offer sacrifice to them as gods, calling Paul "Mercury" but calling Barnabas "Zeus" (Acts 14:8–18)! Well, they saw the power of the Holy Spirit—Saint Barnabas, Apostle and Martyr, may your example inspire, and may your good influence ever encourage, comfort and assist us.

A Foothold on the Future

SAINT LUKE'S PARABLE TODAY is usually called The Dishonest Steward, but it has also been called The Shrewd Manager.[1] A rich man heard his steward was wasting his goods and summoned him to give an account of his stewardship—from which he would be fired. But the steward responded decisively to his crisis. "What shall I do? I cannot dig; I am ashamed to beg." So he quickly reduced the bills owed to his master by substantial amounts, thereby ingratiating himself to his master's debtors. His maneuver was designed "that they may receive me into their houses" and thereby secure the steward future employment. The rich master commended him for this; not for his dishonesty as a steward but for his resourcefulness in the crisis. The steward was shrewd, even wise and prudent as a survivor.

It was customary in the ancient Middle East for loans to be made with interest, on top of which the agent of the transaction added his own fee or commission—like a tax collector acting as Caesar's agent. In this case it appears that the steward, in reducing the bills for his master's debtors, eliminated his own cut.[2]

---

1   E.g., the New International Version (Luke 16:1–13).

2   Joseph Fitzmyer, *The Gospel According to Luke* (Garden City: Doubleday, 1981), 1095–1102.

Robert Frost's poem "Provide, Provide" gets at what the steward did to meet his crisis:

Too many fall from great and good
For you to doubt the likelihood…
No memory for having starred
Atones for later disregard
Or keeps the end from being hard.
Better to go down dignified
With boughten friendship at your side
Than none at all. Provide, provide!

Jesus, by concluding this parable with the rich master's commendation of his servant's cleverness, makes his own moral of the story. He says we are to use "unrighteous mammon" (that is, "filthy lucre") in such a way that it opens doors of houses in the eternal habitations. Make yourselves friends in this way, says Jesus. He means, use money to make deposits in God's Goodwill Bank. Be faithful with the money of this world to inherit the treasure of God's kingdom. You can't serve God and Mammon, but you can use mammon for God.

Money by itself is not evil. But human economy and enterprise, not to mention our love of money, taints it in every way so that it is called unrighteous mammon or filthy lucre. We must use it. Jesus says, use it to do good and win yourselves friends in heaven!

The dishonest steward was faced with a crisis. He was called to account and about to be out on the street. His swift resourcefulness, giving away money that he customarily pocketed, won him a foot-hold on the future.[3]

When Jesus comes into our lives, we have a crisis on our hands as well: a judgment, a change of perspective on all we do and all our relationships. Everything looks different when Jesus arrives. Our families and friends, our jobs, our social affairs, our values and priorities suddenly are brought into the light of Christ and thereby receive an inventory or audit. Furthermore, the crisis is existential: time is short, eternity is long; our life is on the line.

Jesus' Rich Fool a few chapters earlier in the same Gospel (Luke 12:13–21) had laid up riches for himself and was taking his ease, when suddenly God spoke to him: Fool! Your soul is required of you this night! And the things you have accumulated, whose will they be? So it is for those who do not invest in their relationship with God. It was too late for the Rich Fool, but the Dishonest (Prudent) Steward acted in the nick of time. Watch, says Jesus, for you know neither the day nor the hour when your Lord will come.

How many churches, hospitals and schools have been built and endowed, how many good deeds have been performed, by people who got the message and used their money to invest in the kingdom of God! Some of these donors may even have been clever rascals, but they were prudent ones: people who acted in time, or who created gracious surprises in their last wills and testaments.

We are not saved by pure motives. That's a good thing, when you start being honest about your motives. But helping the poor, doing good works, giving money to good causes, opening the hand to the appeal of human need certainly help. These win friends in

---

3 *Ibid.* Thanks to Father Victor Austin for this reference in the Anchor Bible Commentary series.

heaven. Charity signifies a turning toward the kingdom of God and its subjects, so that when time is up and worldly goods are left behind, we may be received into eternal habitations.[4]

Saint Thomas, past, present and future, speaks to this legacy. Here, in the midst of the temples of commerce on Fifth Avenue, people have used "the unrighteous mammon" to open the doors of heaven for themselves and countless others. Here on "Babylon's strand" our ancestors raised this glorious temple of the Lord, this House of God and Gate of Heaven, whose centennial we celebrate this year. For a century Mammon has been devoted to the service of Jesus and his saints on this amazing street corner. Now it's our turn for such devotion. Let's do it while there's time! Let's gain a foothold on the future: provide, provide!

---

4 F. F. Bruce, *The Hard Sayings of Jesus* (Downers Grove: InterVarsity Press 1983), 186–88.

Some Counsel Against Anxiety

*Rejoice in the Lord always...The Lord is at hand. Have
no anxiety about anything.* —Philippians 4:4–13

First, a few words about our author. He was roughly a
contemporary of Jesus, probably younger, although he did not
become a disciple until after Jesus' death. For a while he was a persecutor of the first disciples and known as Saul of Tarsus, a strict
Jewish Pharisee. After he encountered the risen Lord on the road to
Damascus, he became a premier disciple and apostle and was known
as Paul. Transformed by Jesus, he became a virtual cofounder of the
Church as we know it, second only to the Lord himself in historical
importance. Saint Paul made Christianity a universal Gospel and
became the messenger of God's salvation through the cross of Jesus
Christ and of the human heart set free in Christ. His writings com-
prise about half of the New Testament.

Today's epistle, a portion of his letter to the Philippians, was
written from jail. Since Paul was often imprisoned, scholars debate
from which jail he sent the letter, but Rome is the traditional choice.
If so, Paul is on trial for his life and, in any case, he will soon be

martyred with many other Christians under Emperor Nero, who blamed Rome's problems on the growing church. By that time Paul, who was wellborn, a Roman citizen by birth and well educated from one of antiquity's cultural centers, had been disinherited. He learned tent making as a trade to survive. As an apostle, he had nearly been killed in riots, assassination attempts, criminal and civil lawsuits, beatings, stonings, shipwreck and many other dangers. So when he tells the Philippians to rejoice and not to be anxious, he communicates with the authority of personal experience.

There is a vivid second-century physical description of Paul that a number of scholars are inclined to credit. "And he saw Paul coming, a man little of stature, thin haired upon the head, crooked in the legs, of good state of body, with eyebrows joining, and nose somewhat hooked, full of grace: for sometimes he appeared like a man, and sometimes he had the face of an angel."[1]

The Philippians were the first church Paul planted on European soil—in Macedonia, across the Aegean from Asia Minor (Turkey). It started with a bang. Paul and Silas had been imprisoned for disturbing the peace. In the middle of the night, as they were singing hymns, an earthquake broke up the prison cells. Assuming his prisoners had escaped, the Philippian jailer, being a good Roman, drew his sword to commit suicide; but Paul shouted out, "Don't hurt yourself; we're all still here!" Trembling, the jailer asked what he had to do to be saved. Paul baptized him and his whole household (Acts 16:11–40). The Philippian church was generous, contributing to Paul's fundraising effort on behalf of the famine-impoverished mother church in Jerusalem. They also contributed money and sent personal help to

---

1 *Acts of Paul and Thecla*, quoted in *The New Bible Dictionary*, J. D. Douglas, ed. (Grand Rapids: Eerdmans, 1979), 943.

Paul in prison, more than once it seems. Paul rejoices in their faithful support, and in return conveys priceless counsel and wisdom that other churches, such as the anxiety-stricken churches of New York, such as our own beloved Saint Thomas, need badly to hear at this time. So now let us hear it.

To care, as the Philippians cared for Paul and for their fellow Christians, is a virtue, an expression of love. But to foster cares and worries, to fret about things we cannot control, is actually a sin; for it reveals a lack of trust in the Lord. Fretting leads to self-inflicted inward suffering caused by faithless fears and worldly anxiety. Against this, Paul says: Rejoice, for the Lord is at hand. The cure for worry is prayer and commitment to God, in whom we rejoice and to whom we give thanks for life and health, fellow human beings, family and friends, honest work and good conversation. Even more, we give thanks to God in Jesus Christ, who has saved us from our sins and everything that could separate us from God and who by his death and resurrection has overcome the world and all its tribulation. Make your requests known to God in your prayer—for food, shelter, health, work, loved ones, the church and society. Do these things concern us? Then pray to God earnestly each day for them.

I confess that I fall into worry for Saint Thomas and our people in this financial crisis.[2] But then I recall all that the Apostle went through, and I am convicted by his serenity under such hard circumstances and take heart at his counsel. Then I recall the prayers and faith of our forebears here—through fires and financial panics and depressions, through city riots and civil and world wars, through God knows how much tribulation. And now consider: Here is this

2 The autumn of 2008, the "Great Recession."

church, our beloved Saint Thomas, now celebrating this liturgy, hearing Saint Paul's two thousand-year-old epistle conveying the Word of God urgent and relevant in this hour. Behold: a miracle of God's providence! These thoughts take me to my knees in prayer and thanksgiving, where God's presence casts out fear.

The Apostle says he has learned, in whatever state he finds himself, to be content. "I know how to be abased, and I know how to abound; in any and all circumstances I have learned the secret of facing plenty and hunger, abundance and want. I can do all things in him who strengthens me."

The "secret" is that peace of God that passes all understanding to which Paul refers. It "keeps" our hearts and minds "in Christ Jesus." It is a straightforward matter of setting our minds on Christ, on thinking of, by, with and in him. When the tribulation of the world (like the "breaking news" moving across the bottom of the screen on twenty-four–hour cable-news channels) rattles us, it is time to turn off the station, to fast and abstain from the worldly fear, and to focus our minds and hearts on Christ. Nothing has overtaken us that people have not faced in other times and places. These trials are the troubles of the kingdoms of this world. But Christ has overcome this world and offers us a better kingdom, the kingdom of truth, peace, love and eternal life. These are treasures where moth and rust do not consume, and where thieves do not break in and steal. They do not disappear with a stock-market crash and a credit crunch.

The apostle learned these truths from Christ and tested them for decades in the school of life and hard knocks. He replaced self-reliance with Lord-reliance. He says that he (and we, if we will hear him) can learn this peace and joy which you can take with you everywhere, including through death and into the unveiled kingdom of heaven.

I have a suggestion. If you are feeling paralyzed and afraid because of what has been going on, release yourself by making a financial commitment to the church. It is an act of thanks for Christ's amazing performance through all circumstances, and an investment of faith in his Lordship over the present and the future. In the world there is tribulation. But let us be of good cheer; for Christ our Lord has overcome the world.

From Pentecost to Pop Hale

P ENTECOST, WHITSUNDAY, is the third great feast of the Church, ranking with Easter Day and Christmas. You wouldn't know it from the very ordinary attention and attendance Pentecost generally draws. But in the old canons of the Church, in order to be a communicant in good standing, a person needed to receive Holy Communion three times a year: at Christmas, Easter and Pentecost.

One might say that Christmas, with the birth of God the Son at Bethlehem, discloses the First Person of the Trinity as the loving Father. Easter, with the Resurrection of Jesus on the third day after his crucifixion, reveals the Second Person to be the triumphant Son of God, the Word of God made flesh who dwelt among us. Pentecost shows the power and love of the Father and the Son, the Third Person of the Trinity, God the Holy Spirit.

Pentecost is the birthday of the one holy catholic and apostolic Church of Jesus Christ. On the day of Pentecost—as we heard in Saint Luke's account of the day in Acts 2:1–11—the Holy Spirit came down as a rushing, mighty wind, lighting upon the disciples in the Upper Room in Jerusalem in tongues of fire. Had we finished the chapter and gone on, we would have seen Saint Peter, transformed and with boldness preaching for the first time the explicit Gospel of Jesus Christ to the crowds gathered in Jerusalem.

Pentecost is the evidence of the Resurrection, revealing the living Lord as much as his empty tomb. Pentecost is fifty days after Good Friday and Easter. The same political and religious leaders before whom Peter and his fellow disciples shrank, denied Jesus and fled were all still in power—Pontius Pilate, Herod the Tetrarch, Annas and Caiaphas the High Priests. Yet there is Peter, preaching Jesus as the Messiah, indicting the Lord's judges and killers yet explaining that the death of Jesus was the providential plan of God—God's victory over sin—and offering everyone, especially those who rejected Jesus, salvation through repentance, faith and baptism. About three thousand people took Peter up on the offer. All this was the dynamic work of God the Holy Spirit, who changed Peter, empowered his preaching, and moved his hearers to receive the Word.

Pentecost reveals that not only the faith, not only the Church, but God himself is apostolic. The word means "sent." An apostle is one who goes forth on mission, one who is sent. The Trinity is apostolic. Pentecost reveals that the Father sent his Son into the world, not to condemn but to save the world. In the Upper Room on Easter Day, as we heard in Saint John's Gospel today, the risen Lord Jesus said to his disciples, "Peace be with you; as the Father has sent me, so I send you." Then he breathed on them, and said, "Receive the Holy Spirit; if you forgive the sins of any, they are forgiven; if you retain the sins of any, they are retained" (John 20:19–23). He gave his full authority over to the Church with those words. They have been repeated to ordain bishops and priests. The Father sends the Son. The Son sends and empowers his disciples as they receive the Holy Spirit. The mission is to save the world by reintegrating the human race, which has been under the debilitating spell of sin, back into the life of God where it was created to flourish.

A great Archbishop of Canterbury, William Temple, said famously that the Church of Jesus is the one organization that exists for the sake of those who are not its members. That is what apostolic means. The Church was not created to be a club, comfortable as clubs are for the like-minded. The Church is defective if it is not constantly on mission, reaching out to those who are not yet its members, doing everything it can to welcome them.

My former parish, the Church of the Advent in Boston, had a beloved Rector who served twenty-five years, from the Great Depression through World War II to 1960. His name was Whitney Hale. With great affection he was called Father or even Pop Hale by most everyone. He couldn't sing the Mass very well, so he assigned that to a singing curate while he preached. But it was said that he couldn't preach his way out of paper bag. Yet this priest managed to attract many, even Harvard intellectuals, to the Church, to foster vocations to the priesthood, and, in spite of being the Rector of an Anglo-Catholic parish in the center of puritan Boston, he was considered a serious candidate for Bishop in that notoriously low-church diocese. What was it about him? To say the least, Pop Hale was Christ-centered. His own favorite story about his ministry was a day he took the Sacrament to Massachusetts General Hospital, to a retarded man named Jimmy. Father Hale took the Host out of his pyx and said, "Jimmy, this is Jesus." Then he said, "Jesus, this is Jimmy." And so they had Holy Communion. This story, and a comment by a wise priest, helped me figure out Pop Hale's secret. "You always felt in the sweetest, most loving way that Father Hale was after you," said this priest. He was, in other words, always, constantly, aware that he was on mission, running an errand with the Holy Spirit for Jesus.

God made only one Whitney Hale, just as he made only one you and only one me, which is a good thing. Each of us, when we come to believe and follow Jesus, is on call for witness, the sort of thing that characterized that good priest. To be a witness means to understand that we have only so much time—no time to waste but time to redeem—and that we are on mission duty, called to run errands with the Holy Spirit for Jesus. It doesn't mean you will gather crowds, have flames in your hair, speak in other languages and baptize three thousand in a day—although that would be exciting. It doesn't mean you have to be ordained. And it doesn't mean you need a soapbox or a title. You simply must know who you are, and if you belong to Christ, that settles the matter for the witness. There are no lines to rehearse, no scenes to practice. You have only to be willing to speak up, to give a reason for the hope that is in you. God, the Holy Spirit, will give you the right words for the moment. You can do it! It's how God grows his Church.

Pentecost is still unfolding. Saint Thomas and its members are part of the Pentecostal dispensation. Let us bless the time we are given—let us be witnesses for Jesus Christ our Lord. The Spirit of the Lord is with us.

The Athanasian Creed

Jesus said, "All that the Father has is mine; therefore I said that he [the Holy Spirit] will take what is mine and declare it to you." —John 16:5–15

THERE HE IS, the Holy and Undivided Trinity. First in the Gospel text, where Jesus states that all that his Father has is his, and that the Holy Spirit will take what belongs to them, the Father and the Son, and declare it to the apostles. Second, in the invocation of God the Father, God the Son and God the Holy Ghost.

My father-in-law, a Rhode Island fisherman and a person of few words whom I admired, used to say, "When all is said and done, more is said than done." This has been true of the great doctrine of the Holy Trinity, so following that lead I will try to keep to what has been done to reveal this central doctrine of the Gospel. Then I will say just a few things about what is said, in the theology growing from the revelation.

The revelation stems from Jesus Christ. Jesus' conception and birth; his life, ministry, mighty works and words of power; above all his crucifixion, death, burial and resurrection on the third day;

and then his ascension into heaven and sending in his place the Comforter, the Holy Spirit who proceeds from the Father: This is what has been done, what happened in history.

The great Athanasian Creed (which we do not use in worship but which is a historic and authoritative creed of the Church) says that *we are compelled by the Christian Verity [the Gospel of Jesus] to confess each Person by himself to be both Lord and God.* In other words, what we have seen, heard and believed in Jesus forces us to say that the Father, the Son and the Holy Spirit are, each of them, our Lord and God.[1]

This gracious compulsion, this Gospel mandate, can be seen in events like these, and I will list a few. Sometimes it seems that Jesus' enemies, either the devils or the religious people, understood who he was and what he was about more than his friends did. "Who is this that forgives sins?" said the Pharisees. "This is blasphemy!" "By what authority do you do these things?" asked the scribes on behalf of the priests. Or even more, the demonic powers: "What have you to do with us, Jesus of Nazareth? Have you come to destroy us? I know who you are, the Holy One of God!" And when Jesus himself said such things as "I and the Father are one" or "Before Abraham was, I am," these same enemies were driven to a murderous frenzy.[2]

To be fair, his friends were awed: "Who is this, that even the wind and the sea obey him?" Or poor Peter, who staked all his hope on Jesus: "Lord, to whom shall we go? You have the words of eternal life, and we have believed, and come to know, that you are the

---

1 The Athanasian Creed is required to be used at Morning Prayer several times a year by the Church of England's Book of Common Prayer (1662), 27. It is in the Historic Documents of the Church section of the Episcopal Church's Book of Common Prayer (1979), 864.

2 Mark 2:6–7; 1:24; John 8:58; 10:30.

Holy One of God." Christ's death broke their hearts. But when they found his tomb empty, and saw him alive after his resurrection, they worshipped him, and none more than our patron Saint Thomas, who, after demanding to see and touch Jesus' wounded hands and side, cried out, "My Lord and my God." This is the Christian Verity, the Gospel mandate, which compels us to confess each Person, the Father, the Son and the Holy Spirit to be our Lord and God. And the mandate is grounded on the life, the event if you will, of Jesus Christ.[3]

But to return to the Athanasian Creed. It says that just as we are compelled by the Gospel to confess each Person by Himself to be both God and Lord; so at the same time *we are forbidden by the Catholic religion [the universal and ancient faith], forbidden to say that there are three Gods or three Lords.* And what is that universal, historic faith? It comes from God off the lips of Moses, "Hear O Israel, the Lord our God, the Lord, he is one; and you shall love the Lord your God with all your heart, with all your soul, with all your strength, and with all your mind. You shall have no other gods besides him." Jesus himself restated that faith with great force and clarity, just as he worked miracles, taught, and accepted testimony that only God can do, authorize and receive. So the Holy and Undivided Trinity is, to put it plainly, the faith of Jesus and the witness to the Truth of Jesus. This is the fact. The Incarnation of the Son reveals three coequal coeternal Persons in one true and living God. This living God calls us to share in his life by loving one another as He loves us. "The matchless deed's achieved, determined, dared, and done."[4]

---

3   Luke 8:25 et al.; John 6:68–69; 20:28.

4   Hymn 387 (Hymnal 1982).

If Jesus is the incarnate Person of God's Son, the "Christ-event," then the Gospel, actually Holy Scripture as a whole, is the language and literature that tells the story. But where does theology come in, or church doctrine? Theology, said the philosopher Wittgenstein famously, is grammar. The creed and its attendant theology, said the poet and priest John Keble over a century and half ago, "helps to explain the Scriptures, somewhat in the same way, and with the same kind of evidence, as the grammar of a language, once rightly taught, explains the sentences of that language."[5] Grammar helps us understand one another and keeps us from speaking and writing nonsense. Just so, the creeds assist us in communicating the truth of Jesus and prevent us from falling into the misleading error of heresy. Orthodoxy means "true praise" or "right glory."

So it is that the true praise and right glory, the heart of the matter and the gist of the story, are well summed up in these words: Glory be to the Father, and to the Son, and to the Holy Ghost. As it was in the beginning, is now, and ever shall be, world without end. Amen.

---

5   John Keble, *Primitive Tradition* (London: J. G. and F. Rivington, 1837), 141. Cited in my B.Litt. (Oxon) thesis, *A Critical Investigation of the Controversy between Newman and the Tractarians over the Development of Doctrine*, deposited in the Bodleian Library, Oxford, 1973, 7.

Corpus Christi

I TRAVELED TO PHILADELPHIA this past Thursday to preach at the venerable Anglo-Catholic shrine church of Saint Clement's. It was for Corpus Christi, and what they do there is, well, really something. Wrapped in sweet incense and the sublime music of Mozart and Elgar was the Solemn Mass, then the Procession of the Blessed Sacrament slowly around the Church to four congregational hymns, then finally Benediction. We do a version of this within the somber context of the Passion—our beloved Maundy Thursday procession of the Sacrament to the Altar of Repose.

The sight of the Host in the Monstrance touched me: The wafer is displayed, in a kind of bronze sunburst, to be seen. The Rector, under a canopy and in a cloud of incense, carried it slowly, with natural reverence, through the aisles of the kneeling people. I couldn't help turning to gaze; it drew one's "grateful affection." This morning, without the Procession and Benediction, we are about the same business concerning Corpus Christi—we celebrate a feast in honor of the Feast Itself.

A good century ago, when the Anglo-Catholic Movement was making headway not only in the Church of England but in the Episcopal Church and Anglican Communion around the world, there was a mischievous English bishop who wished to put his thumb in the Anglo-Catholic Movement's collective eye. He sent a consecrated Host to a chemist for an analysis of its physical properties. Famously, he published the laboratory's word that there was nothing there of the properties of blood or plasma, of any sign of a human being's physical body. All that was found were the properties belonging to bread. What had the prelate proved?

Whatever glee the bishop inspired in the ranks of the skeptical or irreverent, he had actually demonstrated one side of the mystery of the Real Presence, even of the doctrine of Transubstantiation. That is, that the "accidents," the physical properties of the Sacrament (bread and wine), remain as they are. What he did not disprove, and for that matter cannot be proved or disproved, is the heart of the matter, the Real Presence, wherein the ordinary has been changed into the extraordinary. The "substance," the objective, inner and true reality of the Sacrament, has become the Body and Blood of Jesus Christ by the designation of his Word and the power of the Holy Spirit.

I subscribe to our Anglican Articles of Religion in good conscience, particularly as they have been understood not only in historical context but also by the contemporary Ecumenical Movement.[1] At first it would seem I have a problem. The Article on the Eucharist (Article xxviii) says that "transubstantiation (or the

---

1 The last of the *Tracts for the Times*, published between 1833 and 1841, *Tract Ninety* (1841), by John Henry Newman, was highly controversial for its interpretation of the Articles of Religion and was censured by most of the Church of England bishops at the time, but its method has become widely accepted in ecumenical talks between Anglicans (including Evangelicals and Anglo-Catholics) and Roman Catholics. This is most evident in the work of ARCIC (the Anglican-Roman Catholic International Commission) over the past forty years, especially the Agreed Statement on the Eucharist.

change of the substance of Bread and Wine) in the Supper of the Lord, cannot be proved by Holy Writ; but is repugnant to the plain words of Scripture, overthroweth the nature of a Sacrament, and hath given occasion to many superstitions." The problem with this Article is that it misconstrues the doctrine of Transubstantiation by taking "substance" to mean physical "accidents," scientifically measurable properties. Not so. Saint Thomas Aquinas, who drew up the proper texts of the Mass and the hymns for the feast of Corpus Christi, advanced the definition of Transubstantiation precisely to exclude the error denounced by the Anglican Article of Religion. The Catholic Doctrine upholds the scientific findings of the bishop's chemist on the one hand, while it points to the mysterious depths of Jesus' words of consecration on the other.

When we gaze on the Sacrament, our eyes see bread. But "faith our outward sense befriending, makes the inward vision clear." The little circular Host, the Body of Christ, the wafer held up by the priest and the one placed in your hand in Holy Communion, contains an entire world of grace. The whole Gospel of Jesus is there. We see the Body of our Lord who was conceived through faith in his Mother's womb and born in Bethlehem. We see the Body of Jesus who grew and waxed strong in spirit as a youth and then as an adult. We see the Body of our Savior, who at his Baptism in the Jordan identified with what he is not, sinners like us, and in whose ministry worked wonders, healed illness, confronted evil, drove out demons, gave sight to the blind, restored sinners to fellowship, and raised the dead. We see above all the Body of our Lord who went through his Passion and to his Cross for us, who died, and who was laid in a tomb. And it is this very Body of the Jesus that was not found in that tomb on Easter morning by his disciples but rather revealed to them in appearance after glorious appearance of his Resurrection from the dead. This body and soul, humanity and divinity of the eternal Son, having ascended into heaven, now reigns in glory at his Father's right hand, where he makes constant intercession for us.

And what is most extraordinary is this. On the night of the supreme trial of his life, our dear Lord Jesus took the time to have his Last Supper with his disciples, and to give them the means to have Communion with him, bodily, sacramental Communion, when he took the bread and the wine, and said, "This is my Body which is given for you... This is my Blood which is shed for you."

Before I finish I want to add one more—essential—thing. What Jesus does to the bread and wine, he also does to those who receive it in their hearts by faith with thanksgiving. He transforms sinners into members of his Body, his corporate presence on earth, the living Church of Jesus. We become the gift that we take and eat. Jesus makes our sinful bodies clean with his body and washes our souls with his precious lifeblood, so that we may live in him and he in us. Blessed be Jesus Christ on his throne in heaven, in the most holy sacrament of the altar, and in the hearts of his faithful people.

Good Manners

THE FEAST OF CORPUS CHRISTI, officially The Feast of the Body and Blood of Christ, stems from one of the bright periods of Church history, the High Middle Ages of the thirteenth century in Western Christendom.[1] The natural day for this commemoration would, of course, be Maundy Thursday, but the memory of Christ's Passion on that day makes a separate day to focus on the Eucharist desirable. A devout French nun led a one-woman campaign to have the Thursday after Trinity Sunday set aside for Corpus Christi. She prevailed upon the Pope, who authorized the service of Corpus Christi in 1264.[2] The proper prayers and hymns for Corpus Christi, such as the beloved hymn we sang at

---

1   See the great Jewish scholar Norman F. Cantor's *The Civilization of the Middle Ages* (New York: HarperPerennial, 1994), 565. "The medieval world we know was far from perfect. Life expectancy was short, and disease was mostly incontestable. It was a world burdened by royal autocracy and social hierarchy inherited from ancient times. Its piety and devotion were affected by fanaticism and a potential for persecution. Its intellectuals were given to too abstract and not enough practical thinking. But it exhibited as elevated a culture, as peaceful a community, as benign a political system, as high-minded and popular a faith as the world has ever seen."

2   Dante Alighieri was born in 1265. It was a bright period.

the beginning, were drawn up by Saint Thomas Aquinas himself.[3]

Aquinas's words summarize what we celebrate: "Word made flesh, the bread he taketh, by his word his Flesh to be; wine his sacred Blood he maketh, though the senses fail to see; faith alone the true heart waketh to behold the mystery."[4] This is the Real Presence of Christ in the Eucharist, specifically and substantially, under the forms of the consecrated bread and wine. As Queen Elizabeth I, the architect of classical Anglicanism, reputedly testified, "Christ was the Word that spake it; he took the bread and brake it; and what his words did make it, that I believe and take it."

The Book of Common Prayer requires that the consecrated bread and wine never be returned to common use or treated in a common way. The consecrated elements are either to be consumed or otherwise reverently disposed of, or reserved for the Communion of the sick and others absent of necessity from the Eucharist—which we do at Saint Thomas in the Chantry Altar Tabernacle or in the Aumbry cabinet at the high altar. A white light indicating the presence of the consecrated Sacrament encourages reverence, prayer and adoration. Printed on the back of our user-friendly cards are pastoral directions for receiving Holy Communion. Underlining these directions is the desire to show proper reverence to the Real Presence. Similarly the working sacristy of our Altar Guild is organized around the principle of devotion to the Real Presence, down to the last detail of care for the vessels and linens that are used in the consecration and distribution of the Eucharist. It is a careful

---

3   There is a certified relic of Saint Thomas Aquinas beneath the *mensa* in our high altar. Beside it are relics of Saint Thomas Becket, Saint Athanasius and Saint Justin Martyr.

4   Hymn 331 (Hymnal 1982).

system of reverence toward the great gift the Lord has given us, his own Self, his Body and Blood, for our salvation.

Saint Paul admonishes that we are to be careful on this score. "Whoever, therefore, eats the bread and drinks the cup of the Lord in an unworthy manner will be guilty of profaning the body and blood of the Lord. Let a man examine himself, and so eat of the bread and drink of the cup. For anyone who eats and drinks without discerning the body eats and drinks judgment upon himself" (1 Cor. 11:27ff.). But the Apostle is not just talking about discerning Christ's Presence in the bread and the wine. He is talking about the whole mystery of Corpus Christi, which includes the members of Christ's Body, the People of God. He is speaking about us, starting with our neighbors in the pews here. The reverence shown the Sacrament is of one piece with acts of kindness toward our fellow members and our neighbors.

Eucharistic reverence is a glorious thing. The sacramental devotion evident at Saint Thomas moves and attracts. And this graciousness necessarily reaches out into our fellowship and beyond. The work of the Altar Guild and the acolytes is intrinsically the same as the ministry of welcoming the newcomer and the stranger. Now, buckle your seatbelts: What do we project at our doors and gates? Do we communicate a warm welcome, or cold stiffness? Do we regard "our pew" as our own property, resenting the need to move over for a stranger? If this is what we want, we should consider reinstituting pew rents; but those who would want this wouldn't pay the prices! Here it is relevant to note that generosity goes with welcoming, while stinginess goes with grouchiness. And what about coffee hour? Do we simply hang out with our friends and those we know, or do we welcome the stranger? Coffee hour is an extension of the Eucharist. Rudeness to a visitor is the same as profanation of the Sacrament. Going beyond our doors, the soup kitchen is really an extension of the mystery of the Eucharist, taking food out into the streets every Saturday as a gesture of kindness toward New York's poor. The soup-kitchen volunteers are like the Altar Guild and the acolytes. They all are part of the Corpus Christi. And the soup kitchen itself is a symbol of what should characterize all of us, whether out in the world, at home or at work, on the street or wherever we discover God has led and placed us.

About a century ago, a great missionary bishop in Africa, preaching at an Anglo-Catholic Eucharistic congress in London, said these words to his fellow Englishmen as he spoke of the experience of bringing the Body of Christ to what we now call the Third World: "You have your Mass, and you have your altars, you have begun to get your tabernacles. Now go out into the highways and hedges, and look for Jesus in the ragged and the naked, in the oppressed and the sweated, in those who have lost hope, and in those who are struggling to make good. Look for Jesus in them, and, when you have found him, gird yourself with his towel of fellowship and wash his feet in the person of his brethren."[5] As a young priest studying in England, I met old church people who witnessed this sermon and its potent effects on the hearers. They said it was a moment of a lifetime.

What we do and commemorate today is that same moment: Christ made really present in the holy sacrament of the altar and in the persons and lives of the children for whom he gave his body

---

5   Frank Weston (1871–1924), Bishop of Zanzibar. See *Love's Redeeming Work: The Anglican Quest for Holiness*, Geoffrey Rowell, Kenneth Stevenson and Rowan Williams, eds. (Oxford: Oxford University Press, 2001), 561.

and blood. Let our beloved parish be the place where, in the glory of Corpus Christi, we love one another as the Lord has loved us.

Hail Mary, Full of Grace

I WAS BAPTIZED AND REARED by devout parents in an ecumenically
minded liberal protestant church called The Disciples of Christ.
I look on that upbringing with grateful affection. However, liberal
and ecumenical as we were, there wasn't much that I remember
about Mary, the mother of Jesus. When I entered the Episcopal
Church in college, I began to see images of Mary here and there, but
it was her inclusion in the ancient creeds we use and in other places
in The Book of Common Prayer, such as the prayers and lessons for
today, that got my attention.

The Apostles Creed, which is used at Baptism and at daily
Morning and Evening Prayer, reminds us that Jesus Christ, God's
only Son our Lord, was conceived by the Holy Ghost and born of
the Virgin Mary. The Nicene Creed, which is used at the Eucharist
and which we shall recite in a few minutes, says we believe in one
Lord Jesus Christ, the only-begotten Son of God, begotten of his
Father before all worlds…very God of very God…of one substance
with the Father…who for our salvation came down from heaven,
and was incarnate by the Holy Ghost of the Virgin Mary, and was
made man. That got my attention, and I began to notice some
things about the human side of the mystery of Christ. I noticed

that Mary was, as another venerable creed puts it, the Mother of God, God incarnate, God our Savior; for Jesus did not grow into being God but man—the divine Son took flesh at his conception in his mother's womb; he was God always and from beginning to end. Thus the Word was made flesh and dwelt among us.

Furthermore, I noticed that this wonderful mystery, which we celebrate at Christmas especially, occurred because Mary, at considerable risk, said yes to God. The angel Gabriel conveyed the message about God's Son, that the Holy Spirit would overshadow Mary with God's grace and power, and that she was to be Christ's Mother without human intercourse. The coming of Christ was by the grace of a free will, the consent of Mary. That grace worked further on, with Joseph accepting, believing, and protecting his young wife-to-be. If we are to understand the Person of Jesus Christ, we will want to grasp both his divine identity and those who first received him.

Joseph disappears from the scene in the Gospels after Jesus' youth, and tradition says he was older and predeceased Mary. But Mary was with Jesus all the way, loyal to her Son right to the cross, a witness of his Resurrection and present on the Day of Pentecost in the Upper Room. Her loyalty was tested, like a sword in her soul. She feared for her Son's safety and wanted him to come home at one point. But Jesus had said his true family are those who hear God's word and do God's will. So Mary grew in grace, but come to think about it, she became Christ's mother in the first place by hearing God's word and doing his will. For Christ was conceived as Mary responded to the angel, Yes; I am the servant of the Lord; let it be to me according to your word.

Today we celebrate the whole of Mary's life. Roman Catholics call today the Assumption of Mary, meaning the taking up of Mary, body and soul, at the end of her life, into heaven. The Eastern Orthodox call today the Dormition, or the falling asleep, of Mary, as she is taken into heaven. But this idea is not just Roman Catholic and Orthodox, but classically Anglican and Protestant too. Rembrandt, a member of the Dutch Reformed Church, etched a lovely picture of Mary on her deathbed being taken up by the angels into heaven to be with her Son.

Today's Gospel from Saint Luke (1:46-55) is the Song of Mary. The background: Three months' pregnant with Christ, Mary goes to visit her kinswoman Elizabeth, who is about to give birth to John the Baptist. "How is this," exclaims Elizabeth, "that the Mother of my Lord should come to me?" And Mary breaks into song. That song, called the Magnificat, is appointed for every day at Evening Prayer, or Evensong. Our choir has sung this canticle to hundreds of settings; it is one of the glories of the Anglican choral heritage. One verse is, "For behold from henceforth all generations shall call me blessed. For he that is mighty hath magnified me; and holy is his name."

There is something about Mary, I have discovered, that is more than historical; it is mystical and representative. Mary stands for both ancient Israel (her ancestors) and the Church of Christ (her descendants) in faithfulness, in waiting, hoping and believing. Just as Christ was conceived by faith, literally, in Mary's body, so Christ is conceived in our minds and hearts as our Lord when God's word visits us and we embrace God's will. When Jesus commended Mary at the cross to the Beloved Disciple John's care, he said to Mary, behold your son (meaning John), and to John he said, behold your mother (meaning Mary). And from that hour John took her into his own home. Saint John meant those words to echo through the church and down the generations of belief. It is possible for us to take her into our homes as well, and to have our Lord share with us the graces that he inspired and received back from his mother.

So I have discovered, and I commend this to you as well, that Mary is most definitely full of grace, and that her example and prayers are to be cherished. Christ's Mother is rightly called our Lady.

Hard Sayings, Physical Faith

ALTHOUGH WE TOOK A BREAK to celebrate Saint Mary the Virgin, the appointed Gospel readings for five Sundays running since the last Sunday in July have been from the sixth chapter of Saint John. This begins with the story of the feeding of the five thousand on the eastern, Gentile, shore of the Sea of Galilee. There Jesus perceived that the multitude were about to take him by force to make him their wonder-working king. So he sent his disciples back across the lake in a boat, dismissed the crowd, and withdrew by himself (vv. 1–15).

That night Jesus, walking on the water in the midst of a great wind, met and joined his disciples in the boat, which rapidly and wondrously got to land at Capernaum on the northwestern shore. He then taught in the large local synagogue. The crowd, perplexed at how Jesus had got there (they had not seen him get into a boat or walk the long distance around the lake), attended to his teaching (vv. 16–24). All this is told in the first twenty-four verses of Saint John's chapter six. Then, for forty-seven more verses to the end of the chapter, Jesus speaks of himself in terms of food—namely, as the Bread of Life. "The Bread which I will give for the life of the world is my flesh." In today's portion he is quite graphic: "He that eateth my flesh and drinketh my blood, dwelleth in me, and I in him. As the living Father sent me, and I live by the Father: so he that eateth me, even he shall live by me" (vv. 56–57).

We absolutely need, and are fed by, the sacred humanity, the flesh and blood, of Jesus Christ, the Son of Man. We absolutely need it. Except you eat the flesh and drink the blood of the Son of Man, you have no life in you, said Jesus. Why is this? Because Jesus is far more human than we. Jesus is fully, perfectly Human. By contrast our humanity is marred, twisted and diminished by our manifold sins. The proof is inside us. Why do we blush when we are caught in a lie, or ashamed? Do we feel fulfilled when we hurt, abuse, take unfair advantage of or betray someone, when we leave undone something we know must be done? We do not; and if such things do not bother us, then we are further dehumanized by a coarsened or even missing conscience. Sin subtracts from our humanity. Think of Adam and Eve hiding from the presence of God after disobeying him.

This brings us to the fulfillment of humanity. Free, obedient, constant communion with our Maker is the fulfillment of humanity. Harmony with the word and commandment of God is not servitude. Sin is the bondage of the will. The service of God is perfect freedom. Surrender to God is power. This is the secret of the eternal Son and Word of God who in Christ took upon him our flesh as the Son of Man. Jesus calls himself the Son of Man and means by this the One True Human Being—the New Adam. He once told his disciples, who wondered if he had gotten food, that his food was "to do the will of him who sent me, and to accomplish his work."[1] As we heard today, "I live by the Father."

---

1 John 4:31–34. This is during Jesus' meeting, two chapters earlier, with the Samaritan woman at the well.

So the food that feeds the Son, perfect union with the Father and harmony with his will, animates every fiber of his being, soul and spirit, flesh and blood—especially flesh and blood, because it is his life's work to incarnate God, to be the Word made flesh, and in that flesh to confront and to atone for our predicament, our enslavement to sin. On the cross, out of his pierced side flowed water and blood, the elements of birth and sustenance. When we receive Christ, we are baptized through water into his death and raised to new life with him in his resurrection. And then we are fed, sustained by the food of his sacred humanity, his flesh and blood, under the forms of bread and wine. When Father Spurlock last week said that all of this—the stone and glass in glorious gothic form, the liturgy, the music, the words of teaching and preaching, even the fellowship and service we do as a church—all of this is in honor of the tiny Host, he was spot on (pun intended). God was man in Palestine, said John Betjeman, and lives today in bread and wine, where he gives otherwise dying souls the transfusion of his life.

Many of Jesus' hearers in Capernaum found this offensive: "How can this man give us his flesh to eat?" Even his disciples murmured: "This is a hard saying; who can hear it?" (vv. 42, 52, 60). Jesus' words *are* hard in the sense that they are, and are intended to be, physically realistic. Why? Because we are physical, because sin is as physical as a clenched fist, and the issue before us is vivid. As the Son lives by the Father, so we may live through the Son.[2]

---

2 In the Church's Trinitarian and Christological doctrine (1979 BCP, 864–65), the eternal Son is consubstantial with the Father and coinheres with Him and the Holy Spirit in the Holy and Undivided Trinity; the incarnate Son maintains perfect Personal Union with perfect divine nature and perfect human nature. This eternal life is communicated to us through faith, which is the gift of the Holy Spirit to all who rejoice in Christ's appearing.

Sacramental Communion is not a violent or bloody ritual. The Eucharist is a sacrifice of praise and thanksgiving. Christ's blood-shedding was once for all on the cross. The Body and Blood of Christ in the Eucharist communicate the Lord of the cross, the empty tomb and the ascension to the throne of God. "It is the spirit that quickeneth; the flesh profiteth nothing," said Christ. "The words that I speak unto you, they are spirit, and they are life" (v. 63). In other words, the Son's Objective Real Presence, in his earthly life, his heavenly glory and in Holy Communion, is known and received by the means of faith, which is a gift of the Spirit. Yet Jesus' hard sayings were losing him disciples. He said to the twelve, Will you also go away? Peter, not yet understanding, nevertheless bet his life on Jesus: "Lord to whom shall we go? Thou hast the words of eternal life. And we believe that thou art that Christ the Son of the living God" (vv. 66–69). I'm with Peter; be my soul with Jesus!

We use that quintessential Anglican–Episcopal prayer before Communion, the Prayer of Humble Access: "We do not presume to come to this thy Table, merciful Lord, trusting in our own righteousness, but in thy manifold and great mercies…"[3] The prayer draws from two figures of faith in the Gospels, the Canaanite

---

3 "We are not worthy so much as to gather up the crumbs under thy Table. But thou art the same Lord whose property is always to have mercy. Grant us, therefore, gracious Lord, so to eat the flesh of thy dear Son Jesus Christ, and to drink his blood, *that our sinful bodies may be made clean by his body, and our souls washed through his most precious blood,* and that we may evermore dwell in him, and he in us. Amen." The italicized clause was omitted by the American 1979 BCP. But it has been retained in the Church of England and other provinces in contemporary language versions, as well as in the traditional version. At Saint Thomas we retain the clause (for reasons seen in footnote 5 below) in both Rite One and Rite Two liturgies. It is my prayer that the Episcopal Church will in due course restore the clause for both traditional and contemporary rites and place us back within the classical tradition.

woman with the possessed daughter and the Roman centurion with the dying servant;[4] and it is composed with the theological influence of Thomas Aquinas in the unmatched English of Thomas Cranmer.[5] If its flesh-and-blood language is hard—like Jesus' words in today's Gospel—know that this great prayer plumbs the depths of our human predicament with the soundings of full salvation. It gets to the heart of the matter.

---

4   Matthew 15:22–28 and Mark 7:24–20: The Syrophoenician woman who "wrestles" with the Lord and wins both his blessing and commendation. Even the dogs get the crumbs under the Master's table. Matthew 8:5–13 and Luke 7:1–10: The Roman centurion bids Christ only to say the word, not even to come under his roof. Christ's commends him and answers his prayer.

5   Saint Thomas Aquinas said that the concomitant Body and Blood of Christ (whom we receive totally under each species of consecrated Bread and Wine) nevertheless effectively symbolizes the cleansing and feeding of our bodies by Christ's Body and the washing of our souls by Christ's life-giving Blood. Archbishop Thomas Cranmer composed all these biblical and theological insights in what I believe to be the most superb of all Communion prayers, utterly biblical, evangelical and catholic.

The Difference Between Hell and Heaven

*Jesus said to Judas (not Iscariot), "If a man loves me, he
will keep my word, and my Father will love him, and
we will come to him and make our home with him."*
—John 14:23–29; also Revelation 21:22–22:5

A s much as anything i do I love the Rector's Christian
Doctrine Class, which prepares you for Confirmation and
Reception by the Bishop or just general brushing-up on the teaching
of the Church. And one of my favorite sessions in that course is the
one entitled The Four Last Things.

Traditionally, the Church lists the Four Last Things as Death,
Judgment, Heaven and Hell. Perhaps the order is meant to get our
attention with the last one. But the biblical order, as set forth in the
Apocalypse or the Revelation of Saint John the Divine, is Death,
Judgment, Hell and Heaven. Heaven, not Hell, is the last thing,
which attests to the fact that God, not the devil, has the last word.

In fact the devil is not a counterweight at all to God. He is a
creature, made by God. God created the devil, like all fallen spirits
or demons, to be good, an angel. As I read the Bible, about one third

of these spirits rebelled against God and fell. That is quite a lot, but even if the Kingdom of God were a democratic republic like the United States (which it is not), God, his angels and saints and all other good creatures would have a supermajority to break a demonic filibuster.

If John Milton is to be believed—and I think he's on to something—when the devil or Satan fell into his own self-constructed hell, Pandemonium (the word, invented by Milton, means "All-Demons") he cried out, "Better to reign in hell than to serve in Heaven."[1] If Dante is to be believed—and he surely is on to something as well—the devil spends his eternity frozen deep in hell, chewing on Judas, and Brutus and Cassius (the great traitors against Church and State), his defiant tears filling up the frozen lake in which, by the time of Dante's visit, he was waist-deep. By the way, Dante is the superior theologian/poet here, because Milton makes the devil and his fall more fascinating than he depicts the Lord and his glory to be; but Dante makes the devil what he truly is, tedious and sad. His vision of the Lord is breathtaking, surpassing all loves and passion. Love is Dante's message; and Love is what Christ's Kingdom and Heaven are about.

"If a man loves me, he will keep my word, and my Father will love him, and we will come to him and make our home with him," said Jesus to Saint Jude in today's Gospel. God is Love, and love is what it takes to be at home with God.

In the lesson from the Book of Revelation today, we have Heaven as the last word. Death and Judgment have come. The devil and all his angels, and all who prefer darkness to light, who insist

---

1   John Milton, *Paradise Lost*, 1.263.

on it even as the light comes, all these go into the abyss of their own making. Because God is Love, he does not force anyone to love him. Saint John in his Revelation refers to this in today's heavenly passage when he says that nothing unclean, no abomination, no falsehood, nothing accursed, shall enter into the heavenly city. If we are to live in God's love, we must be all love; there can be no more hatred, or envying, or lying or slander, no more selfishness or cruelty. All love.

In the famous passage from Saint Paul's First Epistle to the Corinthians, chapter 13, the long passage about love (or charity, as it is in the King James translation), the conclusion is "Now we see through a glass, darkly; but then face to face: now I know in part; but then shall I know even as also I am known. And now abideth faith, hope, charity, these three; but the greatest of these is charity" (1 Cor. 13:12–13). Charity, or love, here, comes from the Greek *agape*, which refers to the self-giving, self-sacrificing love of Christ, supremely incarnate on the cross.

We might ask why the Apostle says that charity is the greatest of the three theological gifts, or virtues, of faith, hope and charity. Saint Paul speaks not only about how to live in this life; he speaks at the same time about how it is possible to live in the unveiled presence of God. The reason charity is the greatest is this: Faith and hope, which are necessary for our pilgrimage here on earth, will bear fruit in the next life in terms of sight and arrival. Charity, which is necessary all the way in our earthly pilgrimage, is absolutely, critically necessary once we go to the pure light and life of God. Because if we go to God, and we do not love, we will not be at home; we will prefer the darkness of the other place. But if we have even a little love, God, who is Love, has a little something in us to save and sanctify, something that can be purged and can grow into its own perfection. The devils believe in God (often with more clarity than we do), but they tremble, because they do not love God or anyone else. True faith and hope are tied to love, and they are fulfilled in love's destination.

That destination is quite a place. There will be no sacraments, no Bible, *because we will be there*. The Reality signified and spoken of will be before us—we will be in it. The glory will be that of God Almighty and the Lamb. There will no need for created lights that will eventually go out. The light will be God's and Christ's. The nations will bring in their wealth and glory, and their differences and disputes will be healed. Each month will have a different glorious fruit to feast on. Worship will simply be natural sight, for we will see God everywhere and in all. There will be reunions with those we have known and loved, and very likely with foes as well. There will be introductions beyond imagining, because time and space will no longer separate. And there will be no more death, no crying, and no tears. Those former things have been overcome and will have passed away. Shall we go there, you and I? Love is the way. Christ is Love Almighty. He is the way, the truth and the life.

Grandma's in Heaven

I LEARNED UNCONDITIONAL LOVE from my maternal grandmother. She died forty years ago, and I still cherish childhood memories of hugging and clinging to her. She was "my grandma." But I was only one of nine grandchildren, all living in close proximity in Rochester, New York. Every one of us felt the same way, and still do, about her. Sometimes, half seriously, we would fight over her: "She's *my* grandma!" "No, she's *my* grandma."

Her name was Margery. She was born with the last century in 1900. She wasn't just affectionate, she was self-sacrificing. Her own mother had died at age forty-five of tuberculosis, leaving Margery, the first of eight children, to help her father raise her younger brothers and sisters during their mother's illness and after her death. Margery never went to high school. She worked and then married at age eighteen. Two years later she had the first of three daughters—my mother, my aunt, and one who died very young. Margery's husband, my grandfather, was for the second half of his life an invalid. He called for his wife frequently. During the Great Depression and World War II, to make ends meet, Grandpa built a vending stand for Grandma to sell cigarettes, candy and soft drinks to the men and women walking past her house in and out the nearby factory gate at

Eastman Kodak Company. After the war, when Grandpa stopped working and spent most days sitting in the back of the dining room in the house, Grandma worked full-time on that stand. I kept her company when my family visited, sometimes staying on longer with her. Grandma hauled wood crates of Coca-Cola bottles and soda pop into her cellar from the delivery trucks and later up the stairs and out into the stand for selling. In the winter, she shoveled coal into the furnace. For me this was exciting, but later I realized how hard it was and what a toll it took on her. I cannot recall her complaining; what I do remember are her terms of endearment toward me and my cousins, which to this day fortify me.

My family were professed Christians, Protestants. We went to church regularly. Grandma went with us, but I think when she was alone she didn't go unless someone took her. She liked singing hymns, especially "How Great Thou Art" and "In the Garden."

Grandma's theology was minimal. She thought the Lord was lovely, but she doubted doctrines. When I was first aware of age and death, about 1954, I worried, "Grandma, are you going to die?" "Yes, dear, but not just now." Later, as we got deeper into this: "Grandma, do you want to go to heaven?" I would ask, and some of my cousins shared this anxiety. "You are my heaven," Grandma would respond. She wasn't sure she wanted to fly around forever with a harp; but she was sure about her grandchildren—they were angels right in front of her.

Time passed and we grandchildren went away and got on with our lives. A milestone was when Grandma came out from Rochester to Rhode Island to attend Nancy's and my wedding. By that time Grandma's love for sweets (she had many candy bars in that vending stand) had caught up to her in the form of diabetes, which killed her at age seventy-three in 1973. Toward the end, in the hospital, she scandalized some of my cousins by singing, "Take me out of the ball game."

I did Grandma's funeral. That was hard, but there was a light touch that helped. The funeral home, believe it or not, was named Greaves and Payne. They were partners, Mr. Greaves and Mr. Payne, as in a Dickens novel.

After the service and before the burial, two of my cousins who were of the fundamentalist variety and wondered about my Anglicanism (which I took up in college) asked, "Andrew, do you think Grandma was saved?" Still in my cassock and surplice, I heard myself say, "Well, if she isn't, I'm not sure heaven is for me." They gasped, but I wasn't being irreverent; I was serious.

In today's Gospel (John 13:31–35), after Judas had gone out to betray him, Jesus said to his dismayed disciples, "Little children, I am with you only a little longer. You will look for me; and as I said to the Jews so now I say to you, 'Where I am going, you cannot come.' I give you a new commandment, that you love one another. Just as I have loved you, you also should love one another. By this everyone will know that you are my disciples, if you have love for one another."

The Apostle Paul famously writes, "Faith, hope and love abide, these three; but the greatest of these is love." Why is that? Because when we get there—that is, to the other side of death and the unveiled presence of the Lord—faith will yield to sight and hope will attain fulfillment. But love is the greatest because love will still be necessary to live there, in heaven; for God is Love. Heaven is Jesus' home.

If we do not love we will not enjoy heaven. But God doesn't force us to be there. He lets us be where we can have our own way, forever, if we must. It is not God's will that we die eternally, that we go to hell; but we may if we insist. However, if we have done the works of love, we shall find heaven is lovely.

I believe that when Grandma Margery got there, when she saw heaven, it was a glorious surprise, and that she waits there happily for her grandchildren.

Angels, Freedom, Love

H OLY SCRIPTURE PORTRAYS Saint Michael the Archangel as the intercessor for Israel, the angelic prince of the people of God. Michael's patronage as the guardian angel of the ancient people of God extends in Christian tradition to the "new Israel," the one, holy, catholic and apostolic Church of Christ.

The Revelation of Saint John the Divine that we heard today (Rev. 12:7-12) speaks of a "war in heaven" between Michael and his angels on the one hand and the dragon and his angels on the other, and the expulsion of the fallen angels from heaven. There is a depiction of this conflict between Michael and Satan above the World War 1 memorial in the nave. The Archangel impales the dragon beneath him over the words *Quis es ut Deus*, "Who is like unto God?"—which is what the name Michael means in Hebrew.

An angel is a created, ministering spirit. Since a spirit, unlike a body, is not limited by the constraints of time and space, the angels can move from one end of the cosmos to the other in an instant. Furthermore, the angels, as created ministering spirits, pervade every order of existence and exercise myriad functions. They oversee and prompt the workings of the creation, from the microscopic to the cosmic. Strictly speaking, there is no such thing as an inanimate object, and the angels are involved with it all: thrones, dominions, principalities, powers, cherubim, seraphim, archangels, ranks and choirs of ministering spirits.

All these spirits serve God freely, which raises the issue between Michael and his adversary, "the dragon, the great serpent who is called the devil and Satan, the deceiver of the whole world." This adversary, like everything and everyone else in all creation, was created good. His name, Lucifer, the bearer of the light, indicates original goodness; but his choice was not to serve the Father of lights but to be served, to be the Dark Lord. Through his pride and out of envy of his Maker, Lucifer and the spirits who joined his rebellion exchanged harmony and glory for disorder and ugliness. There was no room for them in heaven.

Where did they go? "Woe to you, O earth and sea, for the devil has come to you in great wrath, for he knows that his time is short." They are here! Then they will go to the abyss. The angelical spirits, good and bad, have an interest in us. They want us to join them.

Here on earth, we go day by day from place to place. Unlike the angels, our decision to serve or to refuse to serve God gets worked out over the daily rounds and the common tasks of a human lifetime. But behind the scenes lies the cosmic struggle, the issue between Michael and the dragon. The greatest literature reflects this, and Holy Scripture states it explicitly. There is much more to life and to the issues of life than meets the eye.

The devil understood this when he tempted Christ, trying to deflect him from serving God his Father. Jesus' faithful mission doomed the devil's cause; Christ's cross is the judgment of Satan, whose time is indeed short and will be all over when Christ returns in glory to reveal his judgment to the whole world.

In the meantime, we have a pilgrimage of faith to walk. We have the assurance of the Gospel of Jesus and the assistance of God's grace, notably animated by the ministry of angels, to resist the temptations and designs of the devil.

We might ask, Why has Almighty God made it this way? Why has God allowed for the possibility of evil in his creation? Why did God create spirits with the capacity of free will, a freedom that included the risk of the great rebellion and the ensuing evil we have seen and that God, being God, obviously foresaw? Why, in the Apostle's words, does the whole creation ache and groan in travail? To go one step further, why has God allowed such flesh-and-blood creatures as we, made of spirit and dust, to be drawn into this contest?

The answer is love. There can be no love without freedom and its risks.

God is great, God is good, and God is free. God chose to create a very good, altogether good, world, and to endow it—angels and men in a wonderful order—with freedom. That is, God made a world that would not only reflect his glory, but at least in the cases of angels and men, could choose to reflect his glory. That is, *to love God in return.*

Free spirits do not have to love God in return. It may be ungrateful, insane and self-destructive not to love God, not to love what God has made us to be, not to love our fellow creatures, but we don't have to. Following Lucifer, it is possible freely to give ourselves to a deadly alternative. God, having foreseen this, has done something more out of love, beyond creation. He has brought good from ill through redemption in the life, death and resurrection of Jesus. God has the care and integrity to involve himself completely in our trials and sufferings, to take them on himself. Christ was manifested to overcome the works of the devil, to make us again the children of God and heirs of eternal life. The "aching and groaning of the creation" is included in God's plan of redemption, embracing everything God has made.

One fine touch of this loving enterprise occurs in Holy Baptism, when we are adopted as God's reborn children. At that time, God appoints for each of us a Guardian Angel to accompany us on our pilgrimage, all the way along to our departure into the life of the world to come.

We live in an extraordinary universe that has been made and redeemed by an extraordinary, loving God. Our world includes not only human beings but also angelic spirits in dazzling array, who traverse the unimaginable lengths of the creation and also involve themselves in what we call our ordinary lives, where we entertain angels unawares. Holy Michael and all the angels, be with us, defend us in the time of trial, and bring us safely into the kingdom of heaven.

The Book of Common Prayer 1662[1]

WE ARE CELEBRATING the 350th anniversary of the Church of England's Book of Common Prayer, which was ratified in 1662. Why? Because BCP 1662 is the rock from which most all other Prayer Books in the Anglican Communion were hewn. Because, even though it can be hard to find in the Church of England, BCP 1662 remains our Mother Church's official Prayer Book and is widely in use in English cathedral worship for Choral Evensong, remaining basic to the musical and liturgical patrimony of our Anglican tradition. Because BCP 1662 contains elements that, like so many phrases in the Authorized King James Version of the Bible (which had its 400th anniversary last year), are permanent gems within English-speaking Christianity. "We have erred and strayed from thy ways like lost sheep; we have followed too much the devices and desires of our own hearts..."

The BCP 1662 was forged in the fires of the Reformation of the sixteenth century and the reactions against it. This was the period of Archbishop Cranmer's move, following the death of King Henry VIII in 1547, under the young and sickly King Edward VI, from quite

---

1 Preached at Nashotah House, Fall Convocation, 2012.

a Catholic Prayer Book in 1549 to a very Evangelical Prayer Book in 1552. Edward died the next year. Then, five years of return to the Latin Mass under Queen Mary. Then, under Queen Elizabeth, the BCP returned in 1559. Elizabeth was the architect of what we know as Anglicanism; her Prayer Book remained until Oliver Cromwell's puritan Commonwealth ninety years later. With a few changes, the Church of England's bishops and the BCP were reestablished in 1662, following the restoration of the monarchy under King Charles II in 1660.

The best illustration, I think, of how all this affected church life is the development of the Words of Administration for Holy Communion in the first three Prayer Books of 1549, then 1552, then 1559 (and of course 1662 and all other Anglican Prayer Books). With BCP 1549, you received, in a Mass that looked in most places fairly like the medieval Eucharist, the Host on your tongue with these words: "The Body of our Lord Jesus Christ, which was given for thee, preserve thy body and soul unto everlasting life. Amen." Three years later, with BCP 1552, in a service that looked very much like the Calvinist services on the continent, you received the Bread into your hands with these words: "Take and eat this in remembrance that Christ died for thee, and feed on him in thy heart by faith with thanksgiving. Amen." Seven years after that (with the five-year Latin Mass interlude), with Elizabeth's BCP 1559, a somewhat more liturgical service was redeveloping in many places such as the Chapel Royal, and you received the Bread with these words: "The Body of our Lord Jesus Christ, which was given for thee, preserve thy body and soul unto everlasting life. Take and eat this in remembrance that Christ died for thee, and feed on him in thy heart by faith with thanksgiving. Amen." The Evangelical-Catholic comprehension was settled.

Thus the architecture of Queen Elizabeth and her bishops, establishing classical Anglicanism. This is the heritage of Richard Hooker, which under King James I and King Charles I received progressive "high church" enrichment. This was the Church of bishops such as Lancelot Andrewes and saints such as George Herbert and holy places such as Little Gidding. Then came the deluge of puritanism in the 1640s. We fast-forward to BCP 1662. Puritan grievances were considered as they had been earlier; most were dismissed.[2] But texts from the King James Bible were added for the Epistles and Gospels of the Eucharist. This brings me to a point: O worship the Lord in the beauty of holiness.

The Psalms and the Canticles in BCP 1662 (and subsequent Prayer Books of the Anglican Communion) are English translations that are fully seventy to eighty years older than the 1611 King James Bible. They are from the Bishops' Bible (the work of Bishop Myles Coverdale) of 1535, which had been the only royally ratified English Bible—these Psalms and Canticles entered the Prayer Books from their beginning in 1549. What is so special about that? These texts are, even when perhaps not as accurate, more euphonious for recitation and chanting than the King James (venerable as it is). Here are only two examples of which there could be many. Coverdale/BCP: from the *Magnificat*: "For he that is mighty hath magnified me; and holy is his name." King James: "For he that is mighty hath done to me great things; and holy is his name." Again, Coverdale/BCP from Psalm 42: "Like as the hart desireth the water-brooks, so longeth my soul after thee, O God." King James: "As the hart panteth after the water brooks, so panteth my soul after thee, O God."

---

2 At the Hampton Court Conference of 1604 and the Savoy Conference of 1661 between the Church of England's bishops and the puritan divines.

The Coverdale/BCP translation is easier to recite and to chant. Why? Because the chanting of the medieval church, with its psalms and canticles of the monastic offices, was still echoing in the souls of the first translators such as Bishop Coverdale. The translators of King James were their grandchildren or even great-grandchildren, and by that time the echo of the old cloisters of England had passed away. This was explained to me by Dean Robert Willis of Canterbury, where they use BCP 1662 for daily Choral Evensong. For the Eucharist for the most part they use the newer rites.

Dean Willis also tells me that in spite of the dire reports we hear about attendance in the Church of England, there is a well attested and persistent surge of attendance in cathedral worship around the English Church, not only for big festivals but for Choral Evensong. There are no doubt a number of factors—transcendence, personal space, musical beauty and, certainly, the clarity and precision of the traditional language.

The BCP 1662 was known to be imperfect even at the time. The long-suffering Bishop John Cosin of Durham, a father of that Prayer Book who endured exile in France during the Puritan Commonwealth, wanted much more. He would have rejoiced in such things as we enjoy in American BCP 1979: a Eucharistic Prayer with an Oblation and Invocation, Sacramental Confession and Anointing of the Sick, the emphasis on the Paschal Mystery, Prayers for the Departed, Marian festivals, and the inclusion of Historical Documents of the Undivided Church along with the Articles of Religion.

So again, why should we bother with BCP 1662? Well, at Saint Thomas Church in Manhattan we have a choral foundation, a residential choir school and an acclaimed Choir of Men and Boys who sing five choral services each week. There is the Choral Eucharist on Sunday mornings; but then there is Choral Evensong Sunday at 4:00 PM, and then Tuesday, Wednesday and Thursday at 5:30 PM. These services each draw (in addition to the choir) between one hundred and two hundred people on average—that is between four hundred and five hundred on average each week in addition to Sunday morning. Those who attend are friends from other churches, workers at the end of the day, tourists, seekers, lookers and wanderers. Evensong, as in the English cathedrals, has grown at Saint Thomas. Fifth Avenue is quite a place, a mall in the middle of the world. We use the BCP 1662 Evensong settings, Coverdale Psalter and Canticles. Why? Because that is what the choral settings, from the late sixteenth century to the day before yesterday, were and are composed for.[3] It's a little like the Greek and Latin ordinary of the Mass for which music is being composed even now, except that it is Elizabethan English. Given what we hear constantly from those all over the country and the world who listen to Evensong on our webcasts, New York City is not the only place where this patrimony is appreciated and loved.

Anglicanism clearly has developed and will develop other forms beyond BCP 1662. Yet that old book, written in the era of Shakespeare, retains a voice that abides in English religion and literature. Its phrases still feed and warm the soul; they are, in a word, memorable. *And because they are memorable, they attract.* We have found, as have the English Cathedrals, that appropriate use of the old BCP has a way of attracting young people and helping with church growth. Listen to what the grandchildren say when they discover

---

3 The Versicles and Responses and Lesser Litany as well as the Magnificat and Nunc Dimittis.

the wonders hidden in the attic in their grandparents' house. They rediscover old things and see them as new, refreshing and delightful. The Good News of Jesus Christ should be just that; and Jesus said that the scribe trained for the kingdom of heaven brings out of his treasure both things new and things old.

The Second Coming

THE CHURCH DESIGNED THE ADVENT SEASON to prepare us for Christmas. At Saint Thomas we give you on Advent Sunday (the first of four Sundays in Advent) the entire season in one service. This way we all get the Church's full teaching about Advent, which means "coming to or toward" us—that is, Christ's coming to and toward us.

Working back from Christmas, we have (1) Christ's advent in his Conception and Birth of the Blessed Virgin Mary, his Incarnation, known at the time only to a few people and the angels; (2) Christ's advent in his public ministry, which climaxed in his condemnation by the religious authorities, his crucifixion by the Romans, and his death, witnessed by many, friends and foes; (3) Christ's second advent in his Resurrection from the dead and his Coming again in power and glory to judge the world, two parts of a single victory which inspired the preaching of the Gospel of Jesus Christ the Son of God, the creation of the Church, and the salvation of all who embrace the Word and receive the Sacraments.

You and I were not of the first, the apostolic, generation who witnessed Jesus' historical death and resurrection. But at the time, Jesus said to our Patron, Saint Thomas, "Have you believed because you have seen me? Blessed are those who have not seen and yet have believed." The risen Lord aimed that blessing at us before he ascended to God, when a cloud received him from the apostles' sight.

But we shall see the risen, ascended, reigning Lord, "for he cometh, for he cometh to judge the earth, and with righteousness to judge the world, and the peoples with his truth."[1] The great hymn we sang at the start is based on the biblical visions and promises, particularly the Revelation to Saint John the Divine: "Behold, he is coming with the clouds, and every eye will see him, even those who pierced him, and all tribes of the earth will wail on account of him. Even so. Amen" (Rev. 1:7).

But what's going on? Wailing on account of him? Yes, wailing— at least at first. Remember that Jesus died for our sins. Our sins, not just the sins of the high priests and Judas Iscariot and Peter and Pontius Pilate, but everybody's including yours and mine—our sins are the nails that pierced him. Salvation is free to us and costly to God, who so loved the world that he gave his only-begotten Son, that whosoever believes in him should not perish but have everlasting life. Those who love the appearing of Jesus realize this; their sorrow is turned to joy, their wailing to singing Alleluia.

Christ has died, Christ is risen, and Christ will come again. This is the only thing that matters in the end, *because it is the end.* It is also the future and the end of time. Then we will have all the time there is, an eternal present, to enjoy the Kingdom of God. For now, we live in the meantime: between Christ's Resurrection and his glorious manifestation to the world, between Christ's death on Good Friday and the day of our death, between Jesus' Resurrection

---

1 Psalm 96:13, the last verse of the Invitatory Canticle for Morning Prayer, the Venite in The Book of Common Prayer, 1928 and 1979.

on Easter and our Resurrection on the Last Day. The Lord *has afforded us time*: time to prepare, to repent, to watch and pray; he gives us time to redeem with acts of love. The poet and priest John Donne, looking to the end, speaks of how to live in the meantime.[2]

> *At the round earth's imagin'd corners, blow*
> *Your trumpets, angels, and arise, arise*
> *From death, you numberless infinities*
> *Of souls, and to your scatter'd bodies go;*
> *All whom the flood did, and fire shall o'erthrow,*
> *All whom war, dearth, age, agues, tyrannies,*
> *Despair, law, chance hath slain, and you whose eyes*
> *Shall behold God and never taste death's woe.*
> *But let them sleep, Lord, and me mourn a space,*
> *For if above all these my sins abound,*
> *'Tis late to ask abundance of thy grace*
> *When we are there; here on this lowly ground*
> *Teach me how to repent; for that's as good*
> *As if thou hadst seal'd my pardon with thy blood.*

Even so. Amen. Come, Lord Jesus.

---

2   John Donne, "Holy Sonnet 7."

Feast of the Immaculate Conception

[God] chose us in [Christ] before the foundation of the world, that we should be holy and blameless before him.
—Ephesians 1:3–6, 11–12

T HIS CHURCH[1] DEDICATES HERSELF on the Feast of our Lady's very beginning on earth, her conception or, more precisely, her Immaculate Conception, and it is that mystery I want to address. The first part of this sermon is a history lesson that will end with the Oxford Movement in nineteenth-century England, climaxing with an exquisite exchange between two great Victorian churchmen. The concluding part will involve some personal application.

The Immaculate Conception was defined as Roman Catholic dogma on December 8, 1854 by Pope Pius IX, who stated that "from the first moment of her conception the Blessed Virgin Mary was, by the singular grace and privilege of Almighty God, and in view of the merits of Jesus Christ, Savior of mankind, kept free from all stain of

---

1 Preached at the Church of Saint Mary the Virgin, Times Square, New York.

original sin." As we shall see, the dogma has correspondents in other branches of the Christian family, including our own.

The belief has had a long and varied history, and has its roots in the early church fathers, who regarded Mary as the "New Eve," corresponding to Christ as the "New Adam." Later Eastern Orthodox fathers extolled the perfect sinlessness of Mary as implicit in her evangelical title "Mother of God," and the feast of her Conception was kept from the seventh century.

I will spare us the debates over the Immaculate Conception in the Middle Ages in Western Catholicism, except to say that it was an Oxford man, Duns Scotus, whose arguments wound up carrying the day. The Western Church Council of Basle in 1439 affirmed the Immaculate Conception as a pious opinion in accord with the Catholic faith.

Reflecting all these developments in East and West, our own saintly Bishop Lancelot Andrewes, preacher to King James and a translator of his great Bible, composed this prayer: "Making mention of the all-holy, undefiled, and more than blessed Mary, Mother of God and Ever-Virgin, with all saints, let us commend ourselves, and one another, and all our life, to Christ our God."[2] This is classic high-church Anglicanism.

So far, so good. Now let us visit the nineteenth century, when the pious opinion was elevated to Catholic doctrine by Rome.

As all of us children of the High Church Oxford Movement revival know, there had been a painful parting of the ways between the Anglo-Catholics and John Henry Newman, who left the Church of England in 1845 to enter the Roman Catholic Church. Newman,

---

2 *The Devotions of Bishop Andrewes, translated from the Greek and arranged anew by John Henry Newman* (Oxford: John Henry Parker, 1848), 93.

after a brilliant career as a pioneer of the Oxford Movement revival, became one of the Roman Church's most able thinkers.

Although Newman's departure was excruciating to his former coreligionists John Keble and Edward Pusey, he remained very dear to them, a cherished and venerated (though separated) friend. And so it came to pass that Dr. Pusey composed a book-length open letter to John Keble in 1866 concerning Anglican–Roman relations. Now here comes our great Victorian exchange.

Pusey entitled his open letter "An Eirenicon," meaning "a peace offering," outlining his hopes for reconciliation between the Churches of Rome and England. Although they were startling at the time, Pusey's points are boilerplate to modern ecumenists in contemporary Anglican–Roman Catholic discussions.

However, concerning the recently defined dogma of the Immaculate Conception as requisite Catholic doctrine, Pusey wrote that it had increased the "substance" of Christianity and constituted "one more ground of severance between the Roman and the ancient Church."[3] This was a grave charge.

Pusey aroused Newman to write his own open letter in response, including a line that deserves a place in the history of wit. "My dear Pusey," he wrote, "excuse me, but you discharge your olive branch as if from a catapult."[4]

But Newman went on. Arguing that the Immaculate Conception stems from the early Church's understanding of Mary

3 E. B. Pusey, DD, *The Church of England A Portion of Christ's One Holy Catholic Church, and a Means of Restoring Visible Unity. An Eirenicon* (New York: D. Appleton & Co, 1866). http://anglicanhistory.org/pusey/eirenicon1.pdf

4 John Henry Newman, *A Letter Addressed to the Rev. E. B. Pusey, DD, on the Occasion of His Eirenicon* (London: Longmans, Green, Reader, and Dyer, 1866.) https://archive.org/details/a678984200newmuoft

as the New Eve, Newman asked (listen carefully): "Is it any violent inference, that she who was to co-operate in the redemption of the world, at least was not less endowed with power from on high, than she who, given as a helpmate to her husband, did in the event but co-operate with him for its ruin?"

Mary, like all human beings, was included, said Newman, in "Adam's sentence" after the Fall. But (listen carefully again): "For the sake of Him who was to redeem her and us upon the Cross, to her the debt was remitted by anticipation." To paraphrase Newman, you could say that by God's prevenient grace our Lady was, as it were, "baptized" at her very Conception.

Pusey was impressed. He wrote a second Eirenicon, and did not send it by catapult! He especially liked the phrase that Mary was immaculately conceived "for the sake of Him who was to redeem her and us upon the Cross." Here was a meeting point, not only for Anglicans and Romans, but for Evangelicals and Catholics.

End of history lesson. What is in this for us, here and now? A great deal.

Mary is the representative faithful Christian. She personifies the Church in her faithfulness, which is why we call her Our Lady. But in her Immaculate Conception, Mary reveals not only the New Eve but also what we are all supposed to be in the first place. God foresaw and chose his people, before the foundation of the world, to be holy and blameless before him, as we heard in the Epistle. In God's eyes, we are destined to be an immaculate conception.

The gift of Holy Baptism connects all Christians to this mystery. Baptism signifies and confers full and entire remission of sin, a fresh start, a new birth, in every sense, won by the Cross of our Lord Jesus Christ. Our Christian life, in which we renew our baptism each day, looks forward to our complete redemption, when we will be free from sin.

If you think of our Lady's Immaculate Conception, and for that matter her Assumption into heaven at the end of her life, what do you have? A "singular grace" to be sure. But in fact this is nothing more than the inheritance of all saints, already realized in Christ's Mother. What we see accomplished in Mary is the fullness of Christ's redemption, the gift that belongs to every one of us by faith and baptism. In this Advent season, when we are particularly thinking of our Lord's glorious return, the resurrection of the body, the last judgment and the life everlasting, this feast of our Lady reminds us that Jesus' victory harvest has already begun. In the words of Saint John the Divine, "Behold a woman clothed with the sun, with the moon under her feet, and on her head a crown of twelve stars." The Woman is the Church, personified by Mary.

Let me finish with the Scottish Episcopal Church's old Collect for this Feast Day: "O Almighty God, who didst endue with singular grace the Blessed Virgin Mary, the Mother of our Lord: Vouchsafe, we beseech thee, to hallow our bodies in purity, and our souls in humility and love; through Jesus Christ our Lord. Amen."

No Graven Images

I̲N̲ ̲G̲I̲V̲I̲N̲G̲ ̲U̲S̲ ̲T̲H̲E̲ ̲T̲E̲N̲ ̲W̲O̲R̲D̲S̲ ̲O̲F̲ ̲L̲I̲F̲E̲ (The Commandments), God gives us Good News. He is speaking to us. He is putting us on the level by showing what a living relationship with him means in terms of our thoughts, words and deeds. *Thou shalt have no other gods but Me. Thou shalt not make to thyself any graven image, nor the likeness of any thing that is in the heaven above or in the earth beneath, or in the water under the earth; thou shalt not bow down to them, nor worship them.* Or, you shall not make for yourself any idol.[1]

Saint Thomas Church is full of images: stained-glass windows depicting mysteries of the faith and saints of the Church; statues of Christ, our Lady and the other heroes of the faith in the reredos behind the high altar; images of Christ crucified and of the angels. Visitors sometimes come in and ask innocently, Why does this church have all these graven images? Doesn't the Bible prohibit them?

God will not have anything come between ourselves and Him. Holy Scripture prohibits, in a strong voice beginning with Moses and running through the prophets, idolatry. Idolatry is the replacement of God with something else, the work of human hands. "They

---

1   Book of Common Prayer, 1979, 317, 350; from Exod. 20: 4–6.

have mouths, and speak not; eyes have they and see not. They have ears, and hear not; noses have they, and smell not. They have hands, and handle not; feet have they, and walk not; neither speak they through their throat. They make them are like unto them; and so are all such as put their trust in them (Ps. 115:6). Then why do we not hire a demolition crew to come in here, and smash and remove all the images? Why are we doing everything we can to restore our beautiful stained-glass windows and to protect our statuary? Because we believe and love *Jesus*—and we want everything around us to promote the worship of Christ, our Lord and our God.

Let's start with Moses himself. In the same Book of Exodus that gives us the Ten Commandments, there are also the commandments, in chapters 25 through 29, concerning the making of the ark of the covenant and tabernacle containing the Ten Commandments, the sanctuary curtains, the images of the cherubim over the ark, the priestly vestments including the sacred lots Urim and Thummim in the priest's breastplate, and the stones symbolizing the Twelve Tribes. There are the ceremonial instructions for sacrifice, changing of garments and burning incense. These various symbols—that is, images—expressed God's coming down from heaven, down to the top of Mount Sinai, down to speak with Moses and write the Ten Commandments, down to dwell with, converse with and lead Israel from bondage in Egypt to life in the Promised Land. You shall be my people, and I shall be your God; you shall be holy, for I the Lord your God am holy. This is a relationship established by the living God—or reestablished, since Adam and Eve disrupted that relationship by disobedience in the Garden of Eden.

That reestablished relationship was fulfilled in the Incarnation of our Lord Jesus Christ, the Word made flesh who dwelt among us and whose glory the apostles saw and preached, bringing it to us. Ever since, the Church has made various symbols and images, icons, of the wonderful mysteries of Christ and of his servants the saints. Are these the graven images, the idols, prohibited by the Scriptures?

The Seventh Ecumenical Council of the Undivided Church, East and West, in 787[2] upheld, against the violence of iconoclasts, the veneration of icons, images and other symbols of the faith— precisely for the reason that Jesus Christ, the Word made flesh, is the image, the icon, of the invisible God: "Have I been with you so long, that you do not know me?" said Jesus, when a disciple asked him to show his followers the Father. "He who has seen me," said Jesus, "has seen the Father" (John 14:6ff.). We have images because God perfected his relationship with Man in the God-Man, his Son, Jesus Christ. Through *Jesus* we have boldness of access to God.

It is no accident that the iconoclastic controversy in the Christian Church took place at the same time as the rise of Islam in the seventh and eighth centuries AD. Islam is radically transcendent, anti-Trinitarian and non-Incarnational; it prohibits even the images of Moses. The greatest theologian of the day, Saint John of Damascus, who defended the veneration of the icons, lived under Muslim rule.[3] John saw where iconoclasm leads: to the denial of God's Son, his Incarnation and his Sacraments. Later puritanism and its image-smashing in the radical forms of Protestantism went the same way.

---

2 At Nicaea, the location of the First Ecumenical Council of 325, which produced the Nicene Creed.

3 From a well-born Christian family, John's father was a tax collector for the Caliph. Paradoxically, John's living in Muslim territory protected him from the Iconoclastic Emperor in Constantinople! Iconoclasm was connected to the Monophysite heresy, which had an inadequate understanding of the Union of the Divine and Human Natures in Christ.

Anglicanism and Lutheranism are right to side with the traditional Catholic and Orthodox churches against this destruction.

We have images of the Son of God and of his Mother Mary and of the saints for the same reason that our principle worship is on the Lord's Day, the first day of the week, rather than the seventh day, the Sabbath, and for the same reason that we hallow and proclaim the name that is above all names: *Jesus.*

To paraphrase the ancient council: The Christian veneration of images is not contrary to the first and second commandments, which proscribe idols and idolatry. On the contrary, "the honor rendered to an icon passes to its prototype," and "whoever venerates an image venerates the one portrayed in it."[4]

When you look at a photograph of someone you love, when you pick up that piece of paper and kiss it, you are not worshiping or serving a paper idol. You love the person whose image you behold.

Our use of icons and images of Christ, our Lady and the saints—together with images of the various mysteries of the faith—leads us on to the incarnate Son. The veneration of the icon does not terminate there in the image, but points and reaches through it to the Lord[5]—in a word, embraces none other than *Jesus.*

---

4 The Council of Nicaea II, quoted in *Catechism of the Catholic Church* (San Francisco: Ignatius Press, 1994), 517.

5 *Ibid.*, quoting Saint Thomas Aquinas.

Christmas Presents

A FEW WEEKS AGO MY WIFE AND I WALKED into the Lionel Train Store on Fiftieth Street between Fifth and Sixth Avenues near Rockefeller Center. The train store is in business only for the Christmas season. There in the window was a brand-new Standard Gauge 2-4-0 steam locomotive, fire-engine red, with a coal tender and two passenger cars. Back from a near-death experience in the 1970s and 1980s, Lionel now produces trains from the templates of their earliest makes from between World War I and II; these are the kind my dad, supervised by his father, had as a child and bequeathed to me in the 1950s and 60s. Standard Gauge is significantly larger than the more familiar O Gauge. But these new models, these tin-plate prototypes, literally have added bells and whistles, and they have steam sounds, hissing and chuffing in the digitally equipped tender, coordinated with the speed of the engine's driving wheels.

I was transported.

Almost sixty years ago, my parents waited for me to get up on Christmas morning. I was three or four, just about the age when our conscious memories begin. I didn't yet know what Christmas was. Finally I came down the stairs. There, ringing the Christmas tree, was an O Gauge 2-6-2 Prairie steam engine with a coal tender, a flat car, a gondola, a coal hopper, a tank car and a caboose. By that time, about 1949 or 1950, Lionel's trains had whistles and smoke pellets. Dad ran it for me till I learned how, and after that, he and I collaborated for as long as I ran my trains, which was into junior high. I am glad my own son is doing the same thing with our grandsons: an apostolic succession of gifts spanning a century! For me, the sound and smell of those trains is the sound and smell of my father's love.

The wonder of Christmas is far greater, I think, than the wonder of anyone else's birthday, including our own, because in Christ we all have a birthday, all of us together. It is why Christmas is so emotional—one of the main reasons, I suspect, that you are all here in the middle of the night. That is also why it is important for the Women of Saint Thomas, and our Angel Tree, to get lots of presents out to poor children. These toys have the potential to evoke awe and delight.

The Baby Jesus received precious gifts from the Magi, the Three Kings, who also made a considerable effort to find and to worship him. But the Child had received amazing gifts prior to those from the Magi. Poor as he appeared in the manger, he was rich beyond imagining. First, his Mother Mary gave him her infinite, immaculate, natural love. Second, Joseph gave him the freely chosen love of an adopting father. Third, the animals gave him the warmth of their bodily presence. Fourth, the shepherds gave him the homage of social solidarity. Then there were the angels, who saw the gifts given Christ from all eternity. Our Lord was very rich already, but he also received tangible presents from those Three Kings. They brought out of their treasures gifts of gold, frankincense and myrrh. Well-chosen gifts, usually the ones we cherish most from those who know and love us best, signify things about us and the donor's relationship to us. So it was with the Wise Men. Gold for a King. Frankincense for God. Myrrh for a Sacrificial Death. In those three gifts, we see the Person and the Work of our Lord Jesus Christ and the heart of his relationship to us. They were iconic gifts, symbolic for all time. And those Three Kings have come to stand for all of us, from every race and language, every people and nation, always, everywhere.

I pray that, as we revisit the wonder, the joy, sometimes the pain, of our Christmases past, we also discover the blessing of knowing who the Baby is: Our King, our God incarnate, and our Sacrifice, who laid down his life out of love for us, and who now lives and reigns for ever and ever.

Three Births

THERE ARE NOT ONE BUT THREE BIRTHS set before us in today's great Christmas Gospel, the Prologue of Saint John the Evangelist (John 1:1–14).

The first birth occurs not in time but in eternity, whereby God reveals himself to be the Holy and Undivided Trinity, first and foremost the Father who eternally begets his Son and is united to him by the Holy Spirit. This is exceeding good news. It means that God is Love, utterly self-giving.

How do we know this? By the light of God's self-disclosure in Holy Scripture. He reveals himself in his creation, whereby he calls all things into existence by his Word or Son, and quickens them with life by his Breath or Spirit. He reveals himself with ever-increasing clarity by the light of his calling of Israel—"writings of the Law, oracles of prophets, music of psalms, instruction of proverbs, experience of histories"[1]—the Word of God written. *Within and fulfilling these written words comes the second birth, the Word made flesh, the one we celebrate at Christmas, the birth in Bethlehem*

---

1 From *The Private Devotions of Lancelot Andrewes,* "Course of Prayers for the Week: The First Day, Introduction," Greek devotions translated by John Henry Newman.

of Jesus of Nazareth the Son of Mary. No one has ever seen God; yet God the only-begotten Son, who came from the heart of the Trinity, he has revealed himself in the person of Jesus Christ. In Jesus we see the human face of God.

Jesus taught us to call God Father. "Abba, Father" is his distinguishing teaching about God. You can count on the fingers of your hands the number of times God is called (mostly likened to) a father in the Hebrew scriptures of the Old Testament, an enormous library of texts spanning two thousand years before Christ. In the New Testament, which is a small epilogue to the Old written in the second fifty years of the first century AD, there are well over one hundred direct references to God as Father, especially on the lips of his Son in the four Gospels.

There is so much else that Jesus revealed, but there isn't time this morning, except to say that he was born to be the Lamb of God who takes away the sins of the world, which means that the day he died, though a terrible indictment of our world, is called good, as in Good Friday, and that God confirmed Jesus' mission by raising him from the dead on the third day after his crucifixion. Jesus' Resurrection is the reason we know him and celebrate his birth.

This brings us to the third birth set before us in today's Gospel—the rebirth of the human person through the birth of Christ in the soul. As the Virgin Mary said to the Angel Gabriel concerning Christ's conception in her womb, "How shall this be?"

How can a person be born again, born from above, after he or she is old (John 3:4ff.)? We can't climb back into the womb a second time. Something else has to happen. It is like the sail catching the wind and moving the boat. It is like falling in love. It is like suddenly knowing who and what you are supposed to be and do, and hopping to it. You didn't imagine, invent, produce or come up with it. It is beyond nature and nurture. It surpasses our willing and understanding. But there it is. It is God-breathed inspiration.

When Christ is received, we are not mutated by magic; we are transformed by grace. We are transformed by the renewal of our minds (Rom. 12:2) to become, in Christ, the people we were created to be: loving, self-giving, generous; forgiving, self-forgetful, sacrificial; faithful, courageous, true; full of hope and joy. Miracles do happen: The blind receive their sight and the lame walk; lepers are cleansed and the dead are raised; and the poor receive good news. *But the physical miracles are signs of something deeper and more lasting that has already occurred in the heart*—the beginning of the journey out of death into life, into Christ, our adoption as the children of his Father through the only-begotten Son.

All of you came here to celebrate the birth of Jesus. But each of us brought some other things as well. What did you bring? What sort of hope or fear came with you? Let me tell you, it is precisely *there in that hope or fear that the word of Jesus is what you need to hear; there that the touch of Jesus is what you need to feel.* Don't be afraid of it. Just breathe in the Spirit and walk. Grow up into Christ. Walk by the Spirit into the kingdom of heaven.

Now to end where we began: There are not one but three births set before us in today's great Christmas Gospel, the Prologue of Saint John the Evangelist. (1) God is Love Almighty[2] from all eternity. (2) Love Almighty came down and was born at Christmas to save us. (3) Love bids each one of us his personal welcome home.

---

2 The phrase is from Austin Farrer's book title *Love Almighty and Ills Unlimited.*

Traversing Afar

Where is he that is born King of the Jews? For we have
seen his star in the east, and are come to worship him.
—Matthew 2:1–12

JUST OVER TWENTY YEARS AGO I sat in his room in the suburban Philadelphia hospital, conversing with the eminent classical scholar Richmond Lattimore, whose translations of Homer's *Iliad* and *Odyssey* were the pride of Bryn Mawr College and remain venerable standards. Professor Lattimore was in his mid-eighties, recovering from an operation.

For decades Dr. Lattimore had attended the church where I was the fairly new rector, going along every Sunday with his devout wife; but he never joined her at the altar rail. It seemed he had certain reservations. In retirement years he had translated the four Gospels, the Acts, and the Book of Revelation from the New Testament, and he had treated us at the church to a charming lecture on the experience of translating Scripture. He had made a point of complimenting the evangelist Saint Luke for his elegant Greek.

In the hospital room our conversation took a turn that brought religious issues to the fore. Something made me take the plunge. "Dr. Lattimore, I know you don't receive Communion, but here I feel remiss in not asking you: Would you like me to bring you Communion?"

"I would love to receive Communion, but I can't," he said with a gentle smile. "Why not?" I said. His smile grew, "You see, I'm not baptized."

This was a revelation. His parents had been Quaker missionaries in China. I remember taking a breath before I asked, "Would you like to be baptized?" "Yes, I would," he said, smiling again. The earth seemed to move. Regarding his precarious health, I asked if he thought I should bring his wife along next time and baptize him simply in the hospital. "No, that won't be necessary; I won't die here this time," he said. It also became clear, now the subject was breached, that he wanted a public baptism in the church, not a private one. It was Lent; I thought, well, why not mention it, so I suggested, of all things, the Great Vigil of Easter Eve. Now with a very broad smile, Dr. Lattimore responded, "That attracts me."

Then I could not restrain myself. "Dr. Lattimore," (though he preferred it, it was difficult for me to call him Dick) "I thought you had reservations about the Christian faith and the Church." "I did," he replied. "But you don't any longer?" "No, not any longer." "Please then may I ask you, when did they go away?" He was silent for a space; then, again with that smile and twinkling eyes, he answered: "Somewhere in Saint Luke."

The great man was discharged from the hospital. The baptism was scheduled and prepared for. His wife was thrilled. The Church as usual was quite full for the vigil service. At the font, it was my turn as celebrant to say to Dr. Lattimore, who was baptized along with an infant, "Do you believe in God the Father…" His turn was then to take part in the Apostles' Creed as his response, but instead, he closed his Prayer Book, clasped it to his breast, closed his eyes, turned his head up, and recited the entire creed with feeling. It was an experience of a lifetime for a young priest to witness. I should add that when the Bishop came to confirm him with our Eastertide confirmands, Dr. Lattimore gave me his emphatic permission to tell his story.[1]

"We have seen his star in the east, and are come to worship him." The ancient Magi used their Gentile arts and sciences to lead them on a long journey to worship the infant Christ. Journeys of that sort can be long; the pilgrims who make them are often changed by their pilgrimage. Dr. Lattimore was in constant proximity to the outward and visible signs of Christ—not more than twenty or thirty yards from the altar rail every Sunday. But long pilgrimages are made in terms of time as well as space, and spiritual distances are such that a few feet can be as far as the east is from the west, and a day can be as a thousand years.

My point is that the journey of the magi is mystical and representative; it includes us all. The Epiphany, the manifestation of Christ, is for all of us, but we each make our own pilgrimage in our own way. The magi, having followed the star, came to the crib in

---

[1] Richmond Lattimore died in 1984. As Rector it was my privilege to conduct his funeral at The Church of the Good Shepherd, Rosemont, Pennsylvania, the Lattimores' longtime parish home. The service was a Eucharist in which all baptized Christians were invited to receive Communion. Dr. Lattimore provided guidance, along with his wife, Alice, in the details of the service, and he encouraged me to tell the story of his baptism in the homily for the benefit of the many members of the Bryn Mawr College community who attended the service.

Bethlehem. John the Baptist, having consented to baptize Christ, heard the testimony of his divine sonship from heaven itself. Mary and the disciples, accompanying Jesus as a wedding guest at Cana in Galilee, saw Jesus display the glory of God in changing water into wine. Richmond Lattimore, the great Greek scholar, discovered Christ "somewhere in Saint Luke."

Every one of us here is on the pilgrimage of life. Christ wills to make his Epiphany, his self-disclosure, to each one of us as his brothers and sisters in the flesh. May God give each of us the eyes of faith to see him.

Domestic Depletion

*When the wine gave out, the mother of Jesus said to him,
"They have no wine." And Jesus said to her, "O woman,
what have you to do with me? My hour has not yet
come."* —John 2:1–11

THE NEW WIDOW was a Christian believer and had been a devout,
sacramental church member ever since her Confirmation as a
teenager. At the age of nineteen she married her husband (who was
twenty-one), and over the decades they became a matriarch and a
patriarch with four children, a dozen grandchildren and to date six
great-grandchildren. She had always had many friends and neighbors dropping by. They had always entertained animals of several
species, inside and outside the house. Now at eighty-two she was
alone for the first time in her life, with reminders of her husband
of sixty-three years everywhere she turned. She had infirmities to
contend with, and she was now struggling through the first year of
a widow's milestones: the first Thanksgiving since his death, their
wedding anniversary, Christmas and New Year. Now came the
nearly thirtieth anniversary of the death of her eldest child, their

son, carried off in a night from his own young wife and children by an aortic aneurism.

It turned out to be a hard day, that recent anniversary of her son's death. She had a cold. A phone call informed her that an old friend had throat cancer. When she hung up the phone, she noticed that her little tropical fish—a gift given to her husband by their daughter in his last days—was floating dead in the fishbowl. She went to bed.

There are several details to note in today's reading of Saint John's Gospel story of Christ's changing water into wine at the wedding feast in Cana of Galilee. Not the least is the role of Jesus' Mother. She and Jesus and Jesus' disciples were guests at the wedding. Cana is in the hill country near Nazareth, their hometown. Wine, like bread, was a staple of life. Wedding feasts could not go on without it. For the wine to give out was a serious embarrassment for the families. Mary interceded; she went to her Son: "They have no wine."

Jesus' response has perplexed, down through the ages. "Woman, what have you to do with me; my hour has not yet come." These words are quietly formal and stern, yet they are not rude or petulant. I believe our Lord is telling his mother that this immediate concern, important as it may be, is not part of his short life's "hour," which is his sacrificial mission and death—something he always foresaw.

Nevertheless, Mary persists in her intercession, telling the servants, "Do whatever he tells you." Believers in the Mother of God's heavenly intercession will see its first earthly instance right here. Christ acts. The drama is understated, but the miracle is awesome. There were six stone water pots each with a capacity of twenty to thirty gallons. "Fill the jars with water," said Christ. They filled them to the brim. "Now draw some out, and take it to the steward of the feast." The steward, unaware of what had happened (only Mary, the servants, and Jesus' disciples seemed to know), compliments the hosts for an unusual grace note: Hosts normally served the best wine first; then, when people had drunk freely, they would serve the poorer wine. But at Cana they had kept the good wine till the end! This, the first of Jesus' signs in Saint John's Gospel, was an epiphany, a manifestation of Christ's glory, and his disciples believed in him.

This story is referenced in The Book of Common Prayer's exhortation at the beginning of the rite of Holy Matrimony. Matrimony, says the old English Prayer Book, "is an honourable estate, instituted of God in the time of man's innocency, signifying unto us the mystical union that is betwixt Christ and his Church; which holy estate Christ adorned and beautified with his presence, and first miracle that he wrought, in Cana of Galilee." When I am preparing couples for the rite of marriage, and often at the wedding itself, I say, Wasn't it a good thing that Jesus and the Church (that is, Mary and the disciples) were included in that wedding? If they hadn't been there, the wine, and perhaps much more, would have given out.

You can run out of a lot of things in a marriage, in a family, in a friendship, in home life of any kind. Domestic depletion includes losses in health, affection, finances, status, setbacks of all kinds; it includes deaths in the family. These losses often cry out for nothing less than miracles, nothing less than changing water into wine.

Mary's intercession with her Son resulted in his mighty action, a demonstration of divine power manifesting that the Word, by whom all things were made, was made flesh, incarnate, in the Person of Jesus. But Jesus had warned his Mother that he had another, more primary concern—namely his hour, which had not yet come. When the Lord was an infant, at his Presentation in the Temple, an old saint had warned Mary that her son's life would involve a sword that would pierce her soul (Luke 2:22–40). Now, at the beginning of his public manifestation and ministry, that sword could be felt in her Son's own words, the mention of his hour. The hour would come within God's definite providence. "I, when I am lifted up from the earth, will draw all men to myself" (John 12:31–33). Jesus said this to show by what death he was to die. Good Friday afternoon was his hour.

The new widow was walking through the valley of the shadow of death. But just as there were reminders everywhere she looked of her beloved husband, so also, if she saw them, were other reminders. There was the little crucifix he had asked for near the end, and her cross, which had two wedding rings on it. A Bible and Prayer Book were on the bookshelf. On the kitchen counter, near the fishbowl, was a leaflet from the past Sunday's Eucharist. Christ would enfold her grief into his own, her hour into his hour. She could rediscover that as she walked through that valley of the shadow of death, the Lord was with her, with his rod and staff to comfort her, even preparing his table before her in the presence of the things that troubled her. These things might send her to bed, but she would most certainly rise again with Christ. It was good that she had included Jesus in her life, and in her wedding invitation, so long ago.

When We Pray, We Are Heard

PRAYER IS OUR CONVERSATION, our engagement with God, by thought and by deeds, with words and without words.[1] It could be as elegant as one of Archbishop Cranmer's collects in The Book of Common Prayer. Or it could be as uncomfortable as a tossing and turning, sweating and pacing, sleepless night. This latter experience would describe what happened to the Patriarch Jacob in today's reading from Genesis (32:24–32).

Jacob was in a tight family squeeze. He had just wrangled with his father-in-law over his desire to have the lovely Rachel as his wife, and now he felt threatened by his own brother Esau's anger over the loss of his birthright to Jacob. Jacob was sweating bullets. And so it was that a "man"—that is, an angel—came, with whom Jacob wrestled all night. No sleep. At dawn the angel put Jacob's hip out of joint and excused himself, but Jacob wouldn't let him go—not without a blessing. So the angel gave Jacob a new name: Israel, which means "one who has power (or has striven) with God and men, and has prevailed." Jacob asked the "man's" name; the angel refused, blessed him and departed. Jacob for his part called

---

1   Catechism, The Book of Common Prayer (1979), 856.

the wrestling place Peniel, "for I have seen God face to face, and my life is preserved."

That was a night of prayer. Not serene and peaceful. Not what we think of as a refreshing retreat. But real prayer, and Jacob lived to tell about it; and the name he gained from it, Israel, is the corporate name of his children and, for that matter, through Jesus Christ and Holy Baptism, the name of the whole people of God, the Church. The Children of Israel: They strive with God and with men, and by God's grace, they prevail.

Jacob's night of wrestling reminds us of Jesus' agony in the Garden of Gethsemane, after his Last Supper with his disciples and before his arrest, trial and condemnation by his own people (the Church) and the State. Sweating blood, Jesus prayed, "Father, if it be possible, let this cup pass from me. Nevertheless not my will, but thine, be done." The three disciples Peter, James and John—Jesus' inner circle—were worn out and could not stay awake. Three times Jesus woke them; three times he wrestled and prayed. Then the answer came: Jesus stayed and did not run away, and Judas Iscariot led the posse to apprehend the Lord, identifying Jesus with a kiss of peace. There was no peace, only the Passion of Christ on behalf of sinners.

True prayer is not necessarily pretty. The beauty of holiness in which we worship the Lord is deeper than aesthetics. In Jacob's case, it means believing in the Lord and hanging on to him for dear life, insisting on a blessing, receiving a new name, and rising from the experience with a limp. In our Lord Jesus' case, it means embodying God's love for human beings and entering the hell of their self-will. While we were yet enemies—of God and of one another—Christ prayed and died for us.

In our classes led by Father Austin, we have recently been studying the Book of Job. Job certainly had a conversation and engagement with God. Job was righteous and devout, yet God allowed Job to be afflicted and to suffer. Years ago, at a Job class taught by yours truly, a young woman summarized what for me has been the essence of the Book of Job, and Job's prayer, in these words: "You're killing me. But I can't live without you."

Jesus, in today's parable of the widow and the unjust judge, tells the story of how the widow, aggrieved by an adversary, came constantly to the judge for justice: "Avenge me of mine adversary." This judge is no Judge Judy; he doesn't fear God and he doesn't care about people. He resembles the bad examples *The New York Post* likes to feature. Yet the widow won't give up. She wears the judge out by her persistence. "Though I fear not God, nor regard man; yet because this widow troubleth me, I will give her justice," he says. Jesus says to us, Hear what the unjust judge says! And shall not God vindicate his own, who cry to him day and night? The point is, we are not to lose heart but to persevere.

Then we might think of Christ's contrast of sinful parents with the Father: Bad as we are, if we know how to give good gifts to our children, how much more will God (Luke 11: 11–13)? When we ask for things in prayer, God, like a good and loving parent, and for his own good reasons, may say no. Or not now. Or let's wait and see.

These answers sometimes hurt or frustrate, but we don't have the full view from our standpoint. We weren't there when God created the angels, or when he set the molecules in motion. But what does happen—as it did with Jacob, and Job, and our Savior himself—is that God has hold of us as we grapple with him. The engagement is transforming, no matter what, and we rise from the experience with a blessing. We may limp, we may be exhausted; *but we have been heard. There was Someone There.* Listen to a man of God speak of prayer:

> *Prayer the Churches banquet, Angels age,*
> *Gods breath in man returning to his birth,*
> *The soul in paraphrase, heart in pilgrimage,*
> *The Christian plummet sounding heav'n and earth;*
> *Engine again the Almightie, sinners towre,*
> *Reversed thunder, Christ-side-piercing spear,*
> *The six-daies—world transposing in an houre,*
> *A kind of tune, which all things heare and fear;*
> *Softnesse, and peace, and joy, and love, and blisse,*
> *Exalted Manna, gladnesse of the best,*
> *Heaven in ordinarie, man well drest,*
> *The milkie may, the bird of Paradise,*
> *Church-bels beyond the stares heard, the souls bloud,*
> *The land of spices; something understood.*[2]

We began with a mention of Archbishop Cranmer's elegant collects, and so we'll conclude: O God, forasmuch as without thee we are not able to please thee: mercifully that thy Holy Spirit may in all things direct and rule our hearts; through Jesus Christ our Lord. Amen.

---

2 "Prayer" in R. S. Thomas, *A Choice of George Herbert's Verse* (London: Faber & Faber, 1981), 27.

Ashes and Bank Accounts

*Lay not up for yourselves treasures upon earth, where
moth and rust doth corrupt, and where thieves break
through and steal.* —Matthew 6:1–6, 16–21

FOR FOUR AMAZING YEARS from 1975 through 1978, I was blessed
to be the Curate for one of the greatest Anglo-Catholic priests
and rectors of his generation, Father John Purnell, at the Parish of
All Saints Ashmont, Dorchester, in Boston. He was six foot three,
weighed from 250 pounds up to what he called his "fighting weight"
at 280, had a brilliant mind for doctrine, sidesplitting wit, and
above all an enormous overflowing heart for Christ's poor. He had
some family wealth, but he preferred to live and serve in his beloved
"down-at-the-heel" cities; before Dorchester, his parish had been in
Paterson, New Jersey.

Father Purnell did not suffer fools gladly, and he did not
let attacks on the faith go unanswered—even (especially) from
persons in high places. One day he and I went to a diocesan
meeting on ministry to the urban poor chaired by the Suffragan
Bishop of Massachusetts—a low churchman who took a dim view

of the vigorous Anglo-Catholicism of our high-church bastion in Dorchester. The day was Ash Wednesday. There were few churches in the Protestant Episcopal Diocese of Massachusetts in those days where ashes were imposed on Ash Wednesday. (One wondered why they thought The Book of Common Prayer calls it Ash Wednesday, but never mind.) Well, into the meeting room we walked, having ridden the Red Line from Ashmont Station up to Beacon Hill after the early Mass at All Saints. We were the only clergy wearing collars and black suits, our foreheads darkly smudged with ashes in a cross. There's no other word for it—we looked Catholic. The Bishop in his natty brown suit and tie shot a glance at us, glowered at Father Purnell and said, "The Gospel today says you're not supposed to disfigure your faces." Without missing a beat, my Rector snapped, "It also says you're not supposed to have a bank account."

We don't put ashes on our foreheads to show off that we are fasting. We receive them to remind ourselves that we are dust and that to dust we shall return. Ashes on this first day of Lent also declare to the world outside that you belong to the Church—an identification the secular world regards with contempt or curiosity. If you feel you must wipe the ashes off your head when you leave here, go ahead. But before you clean them off, consider: Those ashes could provoke a little opportunity to bear witness—as in response to the question, "Why do you have that on your forehead?"

Ash Wednesday is the first installment of Easter, the third day after Jesus Christ was crucified, the day of his empty tomb and his Resurrection from the dead. On Easter morning we will hear the Apostle's words: "Ye are dead, and your life lies hid with Christ in

God."[1] I shall never forget a sermon one Easter morning at Ashmont, when Father Purnell mounted the pulpit and announced to the congregation: "Friends, I have news for you. You're dead. But Christ is risen. Your life is in his hands. Hang on to him for dear life."

All day today people climb the Fifth Avenue steps into Saint Thomas to have ashes smudged on their foreheads. In between services the priests take turns sitting with ashes up here at the crossing. The people make the long walk up the aisle, often stopping to pray first: A man in dirty work clothes, carrying a hard hat. A woman who could be a fashion model. A pregnant mother. A woman who wants you to put extra ashes into a handkerchief to take home to her sick father. A man in a pinstripe suit—he looks like a master of the universe, but when he gets to you for his ashes you notice he has tears in his eyes. A longtime parishioner who smiles and says hi, even as I notice something of eternal longing in his face. A little girl and boy being pushed forward by their mother with her right and left hand behind each of them. A street vendor. A policewoman. They know what the ashes mean: They are dead, dust returning to dust. But Christ is risen. Their life is in his hands. They are hanging on for dear life.

Since our life lies hid with Christ in God, Lent's a good season to make some deposits in that heavenly treasury. Consider some form of fasting, praying and alms-giving. For example, how can one fast from the obsession to be in perpetual Internet and phone contact? "Lay up for yourselves treasures in heaven, where neither moth nor rust doth corrupt, and where thieves do not break through nor steal. For where your treasure is, there will your heart be also."

---

1 Colossians 3:1–4, the anciently appointed Epistle for the principle Eucharist of Easter morning.

Ordination Anniversaries

I planted, Apollos watered, but God gave the growth.
—I Corinthians 3:6–9

S OME MONTHS AGO FATHER AUSTIN AND I noticed that this is a
year of big ordination anniversaries for us. This week Victor is
twenty-five years a priest; in June and December yours truly will
pass fortieth anniversaries as deacon and priest. We decided to
combine them today, with Victor as celebrant and me as preacher.
The Church lectionary's appointed reading from Paul's first letter to
the Corinthians, on the work of different ordained leaders in the
Church, is timely.

On Easter Sunday evening in the year 2000, my son, Matthew,
knocked me over with the news that he wanted to be ordained
(which he now is, and serves as a Rector up in Westchester County).
He said to me, "You haven't exactly encouraged me to do this." I
replied, "That's right. First of all, the Church is a mess and I would
spare you this. Second, even if the Church weren't a mess and things
were swimmingly good, you can't possibly do this job unless God
calls you to it. For a priest to be in harness who is not called, not a

minister of Christ, is the very definition of hell—for the priest and for all around. And besides that, it would be a very wicked thing to push you into the ministry just because it's the family business." He said, "Well, that's what I really want to do, and I feel called to it." With that, I told him I was thrilled, and I am.

The Call is a most forceful prompting from God to preach, teach, minister and in all other things serve the Gospel of Jesus Christ. It makes you hop to it, and you simply have to do it. I had to. So did Victor. The Church discerns such calls, disciplines them, and then authorizes them with ordination. Here we are after all these years, hopping to it.

A few years ago a classmate (Class of 1971) of mine at Yale Divinity School, a Presbyterian pastor, visited me as part of a project he was doing, a paper on those of us still in parish ministry. His question: "After all these years, what has sustained you?" Without hesitating, I replied, "God and Nancy Mead." Then I said, "I need to define a little how God has done it." And without much hesitation four vital elements in my relationship with God—which sustain a priest—rolled out: (1) Mass and Holy Communion on Sundays and major Holy Days; (2) the Daily Offices of Morning and Evening Prayer said either publicly or privately; (3) regular sacramental confession to a discreet and understanding priest; and (4) tithing my income to the Lord. Even though my old friend was a Presbyterian and had some variation of these four points, he knew just what I meant.

The old Book of Common Prayer says it is every Christian's duty to worship God every Sunday in his Church. The Eucharist is the principal service, set up by Christ himself, and it is our air and water, or should I best say our food and drink? It is Christ, crucified and risen for us, the Gospel made visible as a Sacrament. We cannot do without it. We need the fellowship of the Body of Christ; and, except we eat and drink the flesh and blood of the Son of man, said Jesus, we have no life in us.

The Daily Offices of Morning and Evening Prayer expose us to the whole Psalter, all the Psalms, read in appointed rotation, and also the Old and New Testaments, read pretty much in their entirety, year by year, and framed in the prayers of the Church. Saying the Daily Office gives the user a biblical mind, well rounded as the Church reads and sets forth Scriptures as the written testimony to Jesus Christ. It preserves the reader from private eccentricities and heresies. One "goes with the Church" and her ancient heritage. Morning Prayer (Mattins) starts the day: "Open my lips… give me grace…" Evening Prayer (Evensong) offers the day's events and prepares for rest: "Lord have mercy… Thank you…" And one day is as a whole life.

Sacramental Confession, especially for the priest, immerses us in the honesty of what the Christian life is: always repenting, ever forgiven, always dying to sin, always turning and rising to new life. All of us in some way need to confess our sins to God, and "not to dissemble nor cloak them," in the words of the old Prayer Book. Since the priest ministers this life in Christ in many different ways, publicly and privately, in groups and individually, the priest himself (Victor and I, and all your other priests) must be themselves genuine penitents. We must, out of the authority that only personal experience provides, be able to say to you: "Join me… God's grace is very good." In the words of Paul, we must be able to comfort others with the comfort by which we ourselves are comforted.

Tithing also is a matter of the immersion of the priest in ministerial honesty. For me, ever since a beloved mentor witnessed to me about it almost forty years ago, tithing has meant offering back to the Lord, through the Church, the first ten percent of my salary before taxes. That is not a New Testament law, but it does get you into the biblical principle, and the Episcopal Church has affirmed it for a long time. At first it took my breath away, but Nancy Mead took the plunge first and hauled me into the water with her, thanks be to God. And I have enjoyed leading Every Member Canvasses ever since, because, as with Sacramental Confession, I can say "Join me... God's grace is very good." It won't kill you; far from it, you'll find blessings you never otherwise would know. So those are the four points of my quadrilateral relation with God, by which he has sustained me (I know I speak for Victor too) all these years: Holy Communion, Daily Office, Sacramental Confession and Tithing.

There are many things I could say about the "Nancy Mead" part, but I think she'd let me leave it at this (Victor, I think you and Susan feel the same way): God, I should say Jesus Christ, is a present force and living Person in our house. We pray to keep the house under God, and in such a home a relation with the Lord is a natural thing. The kids picked this up through things like grace at supper and night prayers and in conversations. God somehow underlines and punctuates the big things; he's involved. And the children learned it and made it their own.

By the way, did you notice that what sustains a priest is not a sacerdotal secret hidden from lay people? It can and ought to sustain any committed Christian, ordained or not. Just apply it to your own situation as you can.

Finally, from the first promptings of the Call to this moment: joy and gratitude! Christ crucified is risen! He's my Savior, our Savior! The foolishness of God is wiser, the weakness of God is stronger, than the world! Above all, join us in this joy, because your sharing is a big part of it. His service is freedom. My dear brother Victor, how wonderful to serve with you! Twenty-five years, forty years, of Masses, sermons, classes, pastoral conferences, Vestry meetings, Every Member Canvasses, triumphs and pleasures, even the sorrows and pains—God has brought us this far. He has given us a wonderful vocation, job and family of faith. Now let's hop to it and go the distance! One plants, another waters, another harvests, but God gives the growth. And you are God's field, God's building.

The Difference Between Saul and David

The Lord said to Samuel, "How long will you grieve over Saul, seeing I have rejected him from being king over Israel? Fill your horn with oil, and go; I will send you to Jesse the Bethlehemite, for I have provided myself a king among his sons." —1 Samuel 16:1–13

ANCIENT ISRAEL CHANGED from a tribal confederation into a kingdom when the prophet Samuel, at the insistence of the tribal leaders, anointed Saul the son of Kish of the tribe of Benjamin the first king.

Our lesson from the first book of Samuel for today tells the story of how, in the midst of Saul's fairly successful reign, the Lord directed the prophet to anoint young David, the seventh son of Jesse of Bethlehem of the tribe of Judah, as Saul's successor. The first book of Samuel is basically Saul's story; second Samuel is the story of David.

What is the difference between these two kings? God "rejected" Saul. On the other hand, David was called the man after the Lord's own heart. As we heard today, "Do not look on his appearance or the height of his stature...for the Lord sees not as man sees; man looks on the outward appearance, but the Lord looks on the heart."

Why was Saul rejected? Saul had many fine qualities for the kingship. He was tall, strong, handsome and impressive in appearance. He could be courteous, diplomatic and even self-effacing, affectionate and warm, brave in battle, as well as decisive and even ruthless.

Why was David, by contrast, the king after the Lord's own heart? The description we have just heard of Saul could have sufficed very well for King David. What did God see that outward appearances did not show?

Little details reveal the difference between the two men, what Saul lacked and David possessed. Once, in a military situation when Samuel had told Saul to wait for him to offer sacrifice before battle, Samuel delayed. Saul lost patience, took matters into his own hands, and offered the sacrifice himself (1 Sam. 13:8–15).

On another occasion, Saul and his soldiers were preparing for battle with the Philistines. The ark of the covenant had been brought, and while in the midst of prayer, Saul heard a tumult rising in the enemy camp. He interrupted the priest, had the ark put aside, and entered the battle (1 Sam. 14:18–23).

In a word, Saul was a man of the world and was essentially indifferent to religious matters. He used Israel's religion, her prophets, priests and paraphernalia, when it suited him. He thrust them aside, or was irreverent, when they got in his way. Saul valued Samuel's public appearances with him and his blessings, since Samuel was held in awe by the people as a true prophet. But real faith and actual obedience were foreign to him.

The day Samuel left Saul for good, the old prophet told the king, "Has the Lord as great delight in burnt offerings and sacrifices as in obeying the voice of the Lord? Behold to obey is better than sacrifice, and to hearken than the fat of rams... Because you have rejected the word of the Lord, he has rejected you from being king" (1 Sam. 15:22–23). And Samuel went home to grieve over Saul, which is where we find him at the beginning of today's lesson.

With David, it was another thing entirely. For all his sins (remember Bathsheba), David did not use religion for his own ends. He feared, loved and obeyed God. When he sinned, he repented and took the full consequences as his fair punishment from the Lord. Above all he loved the honor of God. God's cause was David's. God's people were David's. David's life had no meaning apart from the Lord. David could not live without God.

Perhaps the differences between the two kings is best put this way. David is the father of the Psalms. His spirit breathes through these prayer-songs, such as the twenty-third Psalm. But it is hard to imagine Saul personally using or understanding the Psalms, let alone composing one. Saul didn't need to; he took matters into his own hands, right to the end, when he resorted to the use of a medium, the Witch of Endor, and then took his own life to avoid capture in his final battle.

The difference between the two kings of Israel, Saul and David, is not very unlike the difference between the two disciples of Jesus, Judas Iscariot and Simon Peter. It is not that one was a sinner and the other was not. It is that one was a believer and the other was not. One used religion because it was helpful or useful for other purposes. The other practiced religion because his heart was in it; it was the outward expression of his faith.

The difference between Saul and David is a deep and abiding difference that continues in the church. It is hard to see on the surface of things. Outward appearances do not, for the most part, reveal it. Respectable, decent, upright people can be seen on both sides of this difference. It is tempting to dismiss the difference between the believer and the unbeliever as not that important.

But it is all the difference in the world. It is the difference between investing all your time and effort in the things of this world or realizing that these things are only indicators of God their maker and are passing away. It is the difference, as Jesus put it, between being rich in the things of this world and being rich in the things of God (Luke 12:16-21).

With Saul and David, the difference showed up in the way the two men approached political and military affairs. We have our own political and military affairs in the great battle of life. We have love, marriage, children and parents, family, friends and companions, enemies and detractors, sickness and death, failure and success, triumph and disappointment. In every one of these critical aspects of life, whether one is a believer in God or not makes an infinite difference.

Self-will is the child of unbelief. Obedience is the child of belief. The issue is, who, or what, in the inmost depths of my heart, is in charge of my life? With Saul, it was Saul. He was the captain of his fate and the master of his soul. With David, it was the Lord. As he himself put it, "The Lord is my shepherd; I shall not want."

Why should we prefer one king, one sort of person, over the other? Whose spirit is the more to be desired? Since this issue is a matter of the inward heart, let us answer this question and conclude by asking ourselves one final question: Who, do you think—Saul or David—was happier?

The Virgin Mother

And Mary said [to the angel], Behold the handmaid of the Lord; be it unto me according to thy word. And the angel departed from her. —Luke 1:26–38

AT SAINT THOMAS WE HAVE GREAT RESPECT for the holy season of Lent. We do not interrupt the Lenten observances of each day or the use of Lenten colors lightly. Only two feasts suffice to break the pattern. The feast of Saint Joseph on March 19 is one. The feast of the Annunciation of our Lord Jesus Christ to the Blessed Virgin Mary, the eve of which we are observing this afternoon, is the other.

The Annunciation is very important, because it is the actual beginning of our Lord Jesus Christ's life in the flesh. The Church calendar places the Annunciation exactly nine months before the date of Christ's birth, from March 25 to December 25, so we see that the Annunciation is the moment of Jesus Christ's *conception* as a human being in the womb of his mother Mary.

"Thou shalt conceive in thy womb and bring forth a son," said the angel Gabriel, announcing to Mary that she was to be mother of the Son of God. "How shall this be," Mary asked, "seeing I know not a man?" "The Holy Ghost shall come upon thee," said the angel, "and the power of the Highest shall overshadow thee."

This is all wonderful, well and good. But one thing remains. Mary was not some passive instrument for God's grace and providence, a mere receptacle for a heavenly child. Far from it.

The great nineteenth-century Danish philosopher and religious writer Soren Kierkegaard meditated on this critical moment in the history of God's providence as he wrote in his journals. He said he could well imagine the angel Gabriel's having proposed the motherhood of God to young Mary, the entire world, the whole cosmos, aching and groaning for the redemption, whispering to her by every means and by all the elements and forces of nature, "Say yes, Mary, say yes."

And so she did, freely. "Behold, the handmaid of the Lord; be it unto me according to thy word." In the words of the great hymn, the "matchless deed's achieved, determined, dared, and done."

Saint Augustine said that Christ was conceived *in Mary's faith.* Through the action of Mary's hearing and her acceptance of the Word of God, the Word became flesh and dwelt among us. Grace met with grace in Mary. God's own Person, God's very Self and Essence, took our nature. But he did so by humbling himself to require the consent of a young unwed woman. That young woman was highly favored, yes. She was full of grace, yes. And by grace she said yes to God. Thus she became the God-bearer, the Virgin Mother of God.

At the beginning of the human race, another woman, Eve, whose name means the mother of all living, said no to God. The medieval Latin writers made much of a reverse play on words. They noticed that "Eva" was the reverse of "Ave," thereby juxtaposing the first mother's no and the second mother's yes.

Eve took matters into her own hands, stepped outside God's grace and providence, ate the forbidden fruit along with Adam, and brought ruin upon herself and all her offspring: self-willed separation from God. She became the mother of sin.

Mary heard the Word of God, asked how it could be, heard again the word to trust God, and embraced God's plan, thereby conceiving Christ and bringing salvation into the world, salvation to all who, like her, were willing to receive God's grace into their lives. Mary became the mother of the Redemption. The early church fathers called her the New Eve. That is why we call her our Lady, and why the Church also calls the Annunciation "Lady Day."

Let me finish with John Donne's sonnet on the Annunciation:

> *Salvation to all that will is nigh;*
> *That All, which is always All everywhere,*
> *Which cannot sin, and yet all sins must bear,*
> *Which cannot die, yet cannot choose but die,*
> *Lo, faithful virgin, yields Himself to lie*
> *In prison, in thy womb; and though he there*
> *Can take no sin, nor thou give, yet He will wear,*
> *Taken from thence, flesh, which death's force may try.*
> *Ere by the spheres time was created, thou*
> *Wast in His mind, Who is thy Son, and Brother;*
> *Whom thou conceiv'st, conceived; yea thou art now*
> *Thy Maker's maker, and thy Father's mother;*
> *Thou hast light in dark; and shut'st in little room,*
> *Immensity cloister'd in thy dear womb.*

Who Killed Jesus?

I BEGIN WITH A WORD about the many references to "the Jews" in the Passion according to Saint John (19:1–37). First and foremost, our Lord was most certainly a devout first-century Palestinian Jew, the firstborn son of a devout Jewish mother. Saint John the Evangelist, a relative of Jesus, was likewise a first-century Jew, as were most all of the first disciples of Jesus. Many of "the Jews" referred to by John believed in Jesus; many also did not, as John makes clear in both instances. When the Evangelist uses the term "the Jews" to describe those who rejected Jesus as the Messiah, he first means the religious authorities who condemned Jesus. Second, his use of the term reflects the experience Saint John and his fellow disciples had in controversies with the synagogues that rejected them as they attempted to uphold Jesus as the Jewish Messiah within those synagogues. The emergence of many of the earliest Christian communities occurred with this conflict.

The conflict between the first-century synagogue and church over the Christian claim for Jesus as the Christ can be seen not only in the New Testament. There are first-century synagogue condemnations of those who deviate from Orthodox Judaism, and the followers of Jesus are on the list.[1] It is a fact of history that Jesus was condemned by the leaders of his fellow Jews and executed by their Gentile Roman overlords. It is a fact of history that Jesus' Jewish disciples were expelled from (split from) their synagogues in the first-century birth of the Christian Church. But we are not in the first century. Subsequent centuries of persecution of Jews by Christians (absurdly—as if responsibility for Jesus' crucifixion adheres to the Jewish people) represent serious misunderstandings, actually terrible betrayals, of the Gospel of Jesus and certainly of Jesus, our Jewish Lord himself.

If responsibility for the death of Jesus Christ needs to be located, we must try to be clear about it. Even as we believers in Jesus are moved by and attracted to the innocence, integrity and love of our Lord, remember that there is nothing very "other" or different from us, nothing especially sinful, about the religious authorities, the scribes and Pharisees, the Jews in various groups or a multitude, the Samaritans, the Syrophoenicians, the Greeks, the Romans or any of the other actors in this drama. For that matter, Saint Peter denied Jesus (three times) just as surely as Judas Iscariot betrayed him. The disciples of Jesus, those who wrote the first Gospels, do not seem to have distinguished themselves. Saint Mark appears to have run away for his life at the time Jesus was arrested, as did others. The women, such as Mary and Mary Magdalene, did better. There were some men, disciples under cover who had to come out in the open for Jesus, like Joseph of Arimathea and Nicodemus, who sat on the very council that voted to condemn Jesus. None of these people, from Pilate to Peter, are a different human species from us.

---

1 Raymond E. Brown, *Christ in the Gospels of the Liturgical Year* (Collegeville: The Liturgical Press, 2008), 150; 183ff.

For the fact is that Jesus' death tears down the dividing wall between Jew and Gentile, just as it tore the temple veil from top to bottom. As the Church grew, Gentiles poured into the Church, overwhelming by number the Jewish followers of Jesus. The Apostle Paul, that strict and particular Jew who once persecuted the Church, after his conversion and several ejections from synagogues due to his preaching of Jesus Christ as Lord became the missionary of Christ to the Gentiles. The death of Jesus and his resurrection from the dead, writes Paul, makes it possible for the Gentiles, in Christ, to participate in what is truly now an international Israel, which he calls the Body of Christ—Israel according to the Spirit, Jerusalem above, which is the mother of us all—of whom all the People of God are elect members.

The barrier between Jew and Gentile has been torn down in Jesus, and we are all one in two crucial ways. First we are all one as sinners. We have, every one of us, fallen short of the glory of God. We are all implicated in the death of Christ. The cross of Christ was not Jewish or Roman. It was made out of sin, our sin. Jesus was nailed to the dead wood of this cross of sin, incorporated into it, so that truly "he who knew no sin was made sin for us." Each one of us has the possibility of playing the part of condemning our Lord. Like the first disciples, we can ask with concern, "Is it I?"

We are, every one of us, in great need of forgiveness and grace. This brings us to the second way in which all of us, Jew or Gentile, are one. We are loved by God. We are, whether we believe it or know it or not, the objects of the love of God manifested in the person and work of Jesus Christ, nailed to the cross and laid in the tomb. "Father, forgive them, for they know not what they do." That love is stronger than death. The grave cannot hold it.

Consider this all personally, for it is personal. Jew or Gentile, high or low, rich or poor, male or female: It is intended for you. He who knew no sin was made sin for you. He died for you because he loves you. His love is stronger than death. The grave cannot hold him. That is why the day Christ died is called Good Friday.

Godforsaken Jesus

S AINT MATTHEW (as well as Saint Mark) tells the story of this
fourth word from the cross. "Now from the sixth hour there was
darkness over all the land unto the ninth hour. And about the ninth
hour Jesus cried with a loud voice, Eli, Eli, lama sabachthani? That is
to say, My God, my God, why hast thou forsaken me? Some of them
ran, and took a sponge, and filled it with vinegar and put it on a reed,
and gave him to drink. The rest said, Let be, let us see whether Elias
will come to save him" (Matt. 27:45–49).

My God, my God, why hast thou forsaken me? These words intro-
duce Psalm 22, which Jesus would have known perfectly, and which
continues with other cries of desolation, "I am a worm and no man;
a very scorn of men and the outcast of the people. All they that see
me laugh me to scorn; they shoot out their lips and shake their heads,
saying, He trusted in the Lord, that he would deliver him; let him
deliver him if he will have him" (Ps. 22:6–8).

My God, my God, why hast thou forsaken me? This is called
Christ's Cry of Dereliction. It often troubles people. How could
Jesus Christ, the Son of God, even in such extremity and pain, utter
such a cry, even if he was repeating the words of the psalm (as some
dying Christians repeat the words of a hymn)?

Or put still more pointedly, if Jesus Christ is God incarnate, the Second Person of the Trinity, the Word of God made flesh, how could he utter such a cry as he passed out of the world? How, why could He be godforsaken?

I believe the answer to this question is hidden in a much wider question of which our particular question is an aspect. The wider question is, Why was it, how was it, that *there was a Jesus Christ at all?*

The coming of Christ into this world is a mystery of God's self-emptying in order to reach us broken, fallen sinners, and to save us. No one has expounded this mystery better than the Apostle Paul: "Have this mind among yourselves which is yours in Christ Jesus, who though he was in the form of God, did not count equality with God a thing to be grasped, but emptied himself, taking the form of a servant, being born in the likeness of men. And being found in human form, he humbled himself, and became obedient unto death, even death on a cross" (Phil. 2:5ff.).

How could Almighty God suffer himself to be a helpless infant in his mother's womb? How could he suffer the limitation of youth and be subject to human parents? How could he undergo the privations and difficulties, the trials and temptations of human life? How could he allow himself to be treated as he was in his passion? How could that happen to him? Why? "For our sake," says the Apostle, "God *made him to be sin who knew no sin*, that in him we might become the righteousness of God" (2 Cor. 5:21).

My God, my God, why hast thou forsaken me? With this cry, Christ takes with him all our cries of godforsakenness. "What is this God?" "Where was God when this happened?" "How could a good God allow this?" "I've had it with God." "I don't believe in God anymore." "It is so wrong." "It must be a mistake." "If this is how God treats his friends, no wonder he has so few." "If there is a God, I hate him." "If God is almighty, he cannot be good." "If God is good, he cannot be almighty." "There is no God."

Christ takes all these heart-cries to his own heart. He takes them, and he melts them down in the fire of his own passion. He unites them to his sacrifice, and he carries them back with him into the heart of God. And Christ, Almighty God incarnate, shows that he has the honesty and courage to take his own medicine. He who knew no sin *became sin for us*. Even to the point of godforsakenness.

Psalm 22 does not stop with godforsakenness. About two thirds of the way through, there is a rescue. "Thou hast heard me!" (v. 21). What was unrelenting desolation becomes continuous exultation in a wondrous deliverance. The psalm ends with ten verses of glory and triumph. Jesus would have known that too, even as his life was ebbing away.

In the earliest days of the Christian movement, the Church had great difficulty not with Christ's Resurrection but with his Crucifixion. How could God's anointed One, the Messiah, how could Christ have suffered such things? Those first disciples had precisely the same problems as we.

Psalm 22 helped those early Christians understand. In it they saw the Passion and the Exaltation of the Lord. It helped them understand that the cross revealed how far down God had stooped to save us. It helped them understand that he declared his almighty power chiefly in showing mercy and pity for us, even to the point of being forsaken by God.

The jeering at Jesus by the onlookers took on new meaning for those first Christians. Saint Matthew saw the significance: "He saved others, himself he cannot save. If he be the King of Israel, let him now come down from the cross, and we will believe him. He trusted in God; let him deliver him now, if we will have him, for he said, I am the Son of God" (Matt. 27:42–43).

My God, my God, why hast thou forsaken me? Dearly beloved, at no point in the entire Gospel is the heart of God more clearly exposed; at no point does God more clearly reveal how much we mean to him. This is what it cost him to redeem us. This is the price he has put on your soul. This is what we are worth to him.

The Resurrection of the Body

Jesus himself stood among them. But they were startled
and frightened, and supposed that they saw a spirit.
—Luke 24:36b–48

I LIKE GHOST STORIES, but the Resurrection of Jesus Christ is not one of them. It's not that Easter isn't a good story. It just isn't a ghost story. It's that there's a lot more to Jesus' Resurrection than the sighting of a spiritual apparition.

Let's start with the teaching of the Church on the Resurrection, summarizing the Scriptures. Article IV of the Articles of Religion in the back of The Book of Common Prayer says it with admirable clarity: "Christ did truly rise again from death, and took again his body, with flesh, bones, and all things appertaining to the perfection of Man's nature; wherewith he ascended into Heaven, and there sitteth, until he return to judge all Men at the last day."

The Resurrection of Jesus is not a ghost story, nor is it the mere resuscitation of a corpse. Jesus raised his friend Lazarus from the grave shortly before Palm Sunday. The chief priests and elders plotted not only to destroy Jesus but to kill Lazarus. A resuscitated person can be killed, can die again. But in the words of the Apostle, "Christ being raised from the dead will never die again; death has no more dominion over him." The same Apostle Paul, in his lengthy chapter on the Resurrection in 1 Corinthians 15, says that the Resurrection, the first fruits of which are seen in Jesus' Resurrection, is a "spiritual body." The Resurrection is beyond our categories; it is a new world.

It is very difficult, perhaps impossible, to harmonize the Easter Gospels. To my mind this enhances the credibility of the witness as a whole. And a picture does emerge that is but a glimpse of the overwhelming Reality that has broken into this world through the Resurrection of Jesus. For the same risen Lord who shows his wounded hands and side and who eats with his amazed disciples also vanishes from their sight. Nor is his appearance impeded by doors locked for fear of the Jewish authorities. And speaking of the authorities, one of their own young agents, Saul of Tarsus, will shortly be turned from a persecutor into a disciple by the risen Lord on the road to Damascus.

That very disciple, who is Saint Paul himself, teaches that the Resurrected Jesus is a spiritual body. In the words of biblical scholar Raymond Brown, "Paul thinks of bodily resurrection, but the transformation indicated by his words seems to take the risen body out of the realm of the physical into the spiritual."[1] Flesh and blood, said Paul, cannot inherit the Kingdom of God. But that flesh and blood has been taken on by God in Christ, nailed to the cross, dead and buried. And on the third day, God raised it up. The Kingdom of God is a New Heaven and a New Earth whose reality is more substantial than anything we have seen or imagined.

---

1 Raymond Brown, *Responses to 101 Questions on the Bible* (New York: Paulist Press, 1990), 75.

The writer John Updike, who died late last year, knew his theology and wrote "Seven Stanzas at Easter" (1964). Updike, who described the foibles of human life in its incarnate details, understood the importance of the Incarnation of the Word and the Resurrection of the Body for a Life Everlasting:

Make no mistake: if He rose at all
it was as His body;
if the cells' dissolution did not reverse, the molecules
reknit, the amino acids rekindle,
the Church will fall.

It was not as the flowers,
each soft Spring recurrent;
it was not as His Spirit in the mouths and fuddled
eyes of the eleven apostles;
it was as His flesh: ours.

The same hinged thumbs and toes,
the same valved heart
that—pierced—died, withered, paused, and then
regathered out of enduring Might
new strength to enclose.

Let us not mock God with metaphor,
analogy, sidestepping, transcendence;
making of the event a parable, a sign painted in the
faded credulity of earlier ages:
let us walk through the door.

The stone is rolled back, not papier-mâché,
not a stone in a story,
but the vast rock of materiality that in the slow
grinding of time will eclipse for each of us
the wide light of day.

And if we will have an angel at the tomb,
make it a real angel,
weighty with Max Planck's quanta, vivid with hair,
opaque in the dawn light, robed in real linen
spun on a definite loom.

Let us not seek to make it less monstrous,
for our own convenience, our own sense of beauty,
lest, awakened in one unthinkable hour, we are
embarrassed by the miracle,
and crushed by remonstrance.

Mr. Updike frequently found his way to the Episcopal Church's altar rail where he heard these words: "The Body of our Lord Jesus Christ which was given for thee, preserve thy body and soul unto everlasting life... The Blood of our Lord Jesus Christ which was shed for thee, preserve thy body and soul unto everlasting life." Let us walk through that same door, receive the Body and Blood of our risen Lord, that our own bodies and souls may be cleansed and prepared here and now and for the Day of Resurrection. The "unthinkable hour" approaches for each of us, and it will come, in a moment, in the twinkling of an eye, at the last trumpet. And we shall be raised incorruptible.

The Day of Jesus' Resurrection

WHEN THE FIRST DISCIPLES OF JESUS found his tomb empty—the stone covering it rolled away and his body gone—they were astonished and dismayed. Jesus had attracted them with his teaching and miracles, his Person and Work. He had also predicted, clearly and several times, his fatal collision with the authorities, his death, and his resurrection on the third day. But the disciples didn't want to hear about his death, and they were therefore also deaf and blind to what he had said about being raised from the dead. It was not until he began appearing to them gloriously alive after his death that they began to take it in, Jesus' Resurrection. This is the event that created the Church as we know it, turned the world upside down with consequences unfolding to this very day, and is the subject of our celebration this happy morning. Those first disciples were in the variations of belief and unbelief found among us today. Jesus Christ died and rose for them and every generation since. He died and rose for us.

In today's Gospel according to Saint John (20:1–18) we hear of Mary Magdalene's report of the empty tomb to the leading disciples, the apostles Peter and John. The completion of Jesus' burial (the anointing of his body) after his death on Good Friday afternoon had to wait until the Sabbath (Saturday) was past—its observance began Friday at sundown. So after the Sabbath was over, early in the morning Sunday, Mary Magdalene and other women came to the tomb, finding the great stone rolled away and the tomb open and empty. Peter and John found it as she reported and observed the linen cloths in which Jesus' body and his head had been wrapped, lying separately in the tomb. It was at that moment that John says he remembered the Scripture and began to believe. Christ first appeared to Mary Magdalene. She initially mistook him for the gardener, but when Jesus called her by name she recognized him and wanted to hold him. He stopped her. "I am ascending to my Father and your Father, to my God and your God." "Go tell the brethren."

"Touch me not. Do not hold me." Jesus after his Resurrection is on a different plane, and the disciples' relations to him are changing. He cannot be held, is no longer confined to time and space. His Resurrection is bodily and spiritual, alive and brilliant. He revealed himself to the other disciples, beginning with Peter. Saint Paul in today's Epistle provides a list of witnesses: Peter, then the twelve, then five hundred disciples together, then James (the Lord's brother), then all the apostles; then lately, Paul himself, who had been a persecutor of the Church.

Consider the condition of the first disciples on that first Easter morning. Their cause had been lost, and most of them had run for cover. The Lord was dead; the Church was dead. Then they found their Lord's tomb empty, and for a terrible moment it seemed even worse: Not even his body was left to cherish and enshrine.

And then Jesus began appearing, revealing his Resurrection, very much alive and beyond the disciples' comprehension. Then the disciples themselves came back from the dead.

Jesus has always been, and still is, ahead of his disciples. When we follow him, our preaching is centered on his Gospel, our worship is his Sacrament, our fellowship is in his name, and our service is in his steps. He died and rose again for all of sinful humanity, and he died and rose again for each of us personally. He did this because he loves us. Jesus proves that God is love. His love bestows dignity and infinite value upon every man, woman and child. God's love conquers all, and it is nowhere more clearly and brightly shown than on the cross. Easter, the Day of Resurrection, shows that the cross is Christ's victory and the defeat of death.

I conclude this sermon with a prayer. I make this prayer because it is our Lord's express desire. May everyone here, by the Spirit of God, come to know our Lord Jesus Christ—either more deeply or even for the first time. May you come to believe and trust in him, and therefore to experience the comfort and the joy of having him be the Savior and Lord of your life, through joy and sorrow and every circumstance, from now on right to the end.

How I Became a Christian

MY LIFE CHANGED FOREVER in college one night—I would not be here otherwise. I was a senior,[1] an American history major; but I could not leave philosophy alone and now here I was up late at my library carrel, studying for a quiz in a religion class. Today's text from Saint Mark was the subject of that quiz in a demanding overall course on the New Testament. Although I had been brought up to go to church by observant parents,[2] I had begun to resent churchgoing in high school though I obeyed my parents' house rules. When I got to college, I stopped going to church and fortified myself with skepticism. But some occurrences brought me to that evening when everything changed.

First, as a freshman I had an argument with a fraternity brother[3] about the existence of God. We were standing on the lawn outside our house. It was a clear fall night in central Indiana. The stars were bright, looked close, and with the moon it was light enough to see.

---

1 Class of 1968, DePauw University, Greencastle, Indiana. Since this story is about how I became a Christian and a priest, elements of it have been in many sermons; this is my first full account of that evening.

2 In a liberal protestant denomination, The Disciples of Christ (The Christian Church).

3 Delta Chi.

"Andy, just stop it," my friend said. "You know perfectly well there is a God." The night sky without words seemed to say Amen: "The heavens declare the glory of God, and the firmament showeth his handiwork...there is neither speech nor language, but their voices are heard among them" (Ps. 19:1–3).

Second, it was the late 1960s. I was involved in the New Left student politics of the day: against the Vietnam War, for civil rights and social justice. All these concerns left me searching for moral anchorage: What, beyond being politically correct, was the meaning and purpose of one's singular personal life? I studied ethics and began to think that a reasonable person could believe in a God— whether I did was still at issue.

Third, I read a short story called "The Wall" by the existentialist philosopher Jean-Paul Sartre. It is told by a political prisoner lying in a dungeon where he will die. The dungeon is an image of life over against death—death, which in Sartre's view is the nothingness rendering life absurd. Facing oblivion, the narrator courageously asserts himself—his beliefs, his actions that have brought him to this end— in the teeth of his prison house and death. One is left moved by his integrity and freedom, exercised in spite of his coming annihilation.

There was one other crucial thing—an experience I had as a boy. My father took me to a movie about the death of Jesus one Lent in a local Lutheran church. This movie's realistic portrayal of the crucifixion shocked me. "How could they do that to him?" I cried to Dad. "All he wanted to do was good! How could they do that?"

All these things just mentioned were at work in me, beneath the surface, as I walked to the college library that night to study for my quiz.

Well, I read my text, which is our Gospel today from Saint Mark (8:27–38). There was Jesus' clear teaching that the Son of Man (his self-reference) must suffer many things, be rejected by the authorities, be killed, and after three days rise again. I didn't attend to that last part, his Resurrection. Then there was Peter, rebuking Jesus for saying such terrible things, and this was followed by Jesus' fierce rebuke of Peter: "Get behind me, Satan, for thou savourest not the things that be of God, but the things that be of men." Then came Jesus' teaching, that if we want to be his disciples, we must take up our own cross and follow him.

Then time stopped. *"For whosoever will save his life will lose it; but whosoever shall lose his life for my sake and the gospel's, the same shall save it. For what shall it profit a man, if he shall gain the whole world, and lose his own soul? Or what shall a man give in exchange for his soul?"*

I had heard these words many times, but their force and meaning had escaped me. Now I saw and knew. First I saw the image of our Lord crucified. It was as though that old Passion movie was rerun before me in my library carrel. I thought, Sartre has nothing over the stark realism of Jesus himself. The prisoner in "The Wall" reflects the crucifix, except that Jesus, God's Son on mission, goes to his death taking on our godforsakenness. Jesus is the embodiment of his own word: Rather than save his life, he loses it, and he wins by losing.

As I lost track of the time and considered the image of that crucifix, I saw that Christ crucified is far more than the tragedy of the human predicament. Christ's cross is Absolute Good News. I also knew Jesus was present—there, *alive*, putting his case to me. As a child, I had thought naturally how appalling the crucifixion is. Now I saw this is Jesus' finest hour, his glorious victory. God's foolishness is wiser than human wisdom; God's weakness is stronger than human strength. I saw, and knew: *Jesus lives.* On the third day he rose again from the dead. I had seen the glory of God up close—in the face of Jesus Christ our Lord.

The library was closing; it was time to pack up and go home. I left the building a different person than when I entered. I had taken the course to study the historical documents of an influential institution, the Church, which I didn't much like. I had always retained a personal attachment to the figure of Jesus—I had never let go of that. But now he had reintroduced himself to me, and it wasn't long before things began to happen.

One Sunday, for the first time in my life, I got up on my own to attend the local Episcopal church (our class professor[4] was an Episcopal priest). I experienced my first traditional Eucharist and took Communion. I began to believe in miracles and in Holy Scripture as the Word of God. Some friends found my churchgoing at best quaint, at worst deplorable. The class professor and the local rector approached me to say they wanted to take me to the Bishop in Indianapolis—they thought I should consider ordination. This happened as I was thinking, *This word of the cross seems crazy, but it's true, and it's the best news in the world; and I am going to do what I can to make it known.*

If I had thought it would lead me here, I might have run away. But God shows us only what we need to know and takes us step by step on the way of the cross. Paradoxically, the cross is the way to life, and joy, and peace. Praise be to thee, Lord Christ.

---

4 The Rev'd Dr. H. John Eigenbrodt, a longtime and well respected professor at DePauw, now deceased.

The Homecoming

WE ARE IN ASCENSIONTIDE. ASCENSION DAY, which was last Thursday, is forty days after Easter Day.[1] During those forty days since the discovery of his empty tomb, Christ revealed his Resurrection to his disciples in many ways. He showed them that he had been raised in a spiritual body. He showed them his wounded hands and side. He appeared in their midst when they had locked the door for safety. He ate and drank with them. He walked with them, taught them that it was necessary for the Christ to suffer and die before entering into his glory, broke bread with them, and vanished. They saw him in Jerusalem. Then they saw him in Galilee. He appeared to individuals. He appeared to five hundred disciples at one time.[2] Finally, in a climactic appearance, he commissioned them to wait for the coming of the Spirit and then to preach the Gospel to the world and baptize the nations in the name of the Father and of the Son and of the Holy Spirit. That was at the time of his Ascension. The Spirit descended ten days later, fifty days after Easter Day, on Pentecost, which we shall celebrate next Sunday.

---

1   This accords with Saint Luke's Gospel and his Book of the Acts of the Apostles.

2   See not only the four Gospels but also Acts and 1 Corinthians 15:1ff.

Where was Jesus, the risen Lord, in between these appearances to his disciples? He didn't rent a room in Jerusalem, and he wasn't staying—as he once did—in Peter's house in Galilee. He was ascended at the right hand of the Father, the place of power and judgment in God's reign. The disciples experienced the Lord's Resurrection and Ascension, and the Descent of the Spirit, as a sequence in time. Yet these mysteries, following Christ's death on the cross, are one, one whole move of grace, and they constitute the Good News of the Gospel, which has created the Church to this day.

When I was boy and was first taught some of these things, I thought the Ascension was a bad deal. I thought, God gets Jesus, and we get the Church. No deal. The first disciples seem to have thought something like this. But Jesus said, it is good for you that I go away; for then the Holy Spirit, the Comforter, will come to you and lead you into all truth. Jesus as ever is right and true. Had the Ascension and the Descent of the Spirit not happened, history would be very different; and we would not know the Gospel. We would not be at all. The Ascension is very Good News.

We have already seen that without the Ascension and Christ's consequent replacement of his bodily presence by the Holy Spirit, the world, we ourselves, would not know Christ. But the Spirit transformed the disciples to preach and teach the nations, to baptize them into Christ, to heal and drive out evil, and to celebrate the Sacraments. Christ's visibility by the Spirit has passed to the Word and Sacraments of the Gospel, to the fellowship and service of the Church, which is his visible Body. The more faithful the Church is to Christ, the more the Body manifests the will of the Head.

But God has done something himself, in himself and for us, in Christ's Ascension. The Ascension completes what was begun in the body of the Virgin Mary, then at Christmas, and then all through Jesus' life and work, climaxing in his Passion. In all this God has prepared a place for us within himself. He has taken our humanity home, right into the Trinity, in Jesus Christ. The Son has completed his mission, his Incarnation and solidarity with us, his atonement for our sins, his victory over our death. He has repaired the breach and ended the exile we began for ourselves with our sins. We think of the Ascension as up, but it is also deep, deep into the heart of God, who transcends all time and space, and yet now has prepared a place, a home, for us. We call it heaven. In the world we have tribulation. There we will have peace and joy. In the world we are exiles and strangers; in God we are home, and by faith we have begun our pilgrimage to that home.

When we pray "through Jesus Christ our Lord," we are literally calling home. We are laying claim to Jesus' place in the heart of God, to the eternal Son who has finished his journey from heaven into our faraway country, like a shepherd seeking his sheep, to bring us home to safety.

In today's Gospel (John 17:6–19), Jesus prays his high priestly prayer to the Father. He is with his disciples in the Upper Room on the eve of his crucifixion. He says he is returning to the Father. Concerning his disciples, he prays that they, and we with them, will be one as he and the Father are one. He prays not that his followers will be taken out of the world but that they will be kept from evil and the Evil One (the devil). He prays that we will make our pilgrimage faithfully home to him and that when we get there, we will share his joy and our joy will be complete. In today's lesson from Acts (1:15–17, 21–26), following Jesus' Ascension, we see the apostles preparing for just that, praying and waiting for the Spirit to begin the Pentecostal dispensation—a time that includes us here and now and that runs till Christ's glorious return to judge the world.

"God put his power to work in Christ, when he raised him from the dead and seated him at his right hand in the heavenly places, far above all rule and authority and power and dominion, and above every name that is named, not only in this age but in the age to come. And he has put all things under his feet and has made him the head over all things for the church, which is his body, the fullness of him who fills all in all" (Eph. 1:19–23 NRSV).

No one likes partings from those we love. As a boy I remember leaving my grandmother. As our car pulled away, I looked out the rear window and saw her standing there, waving and crying. I cried, too. As a child, and then again as an adult, I found peace and comfort in Jesus. I had difficulty with the crucifixion; I thought it was terrible. It is. I certainly didn't care for the exchange, the parting: Jesus goes to God, and we are left with the Church. But then as an adult I came to see the cross is the climax of Jesus' mission of love. It is the price of our passage home. The exchange, the Ascension, is a good deal by a good God. It shows God is Love.

Five Things to Remember

THE SERMON TODAY BY TRADITION is to be for the eighth grade boys who are now graduating as the class of 1997 of Saint Thomas Choir School. They had their commencement exercises yesterday, so they are now officially headed for high school. We have with us today not only these fine young gentlemen, but also their parents, families and friends, and many members of the Choir School community: the school faculty and church vestry in procession, alumni of the school joining the choir, and other good friends of the school in attendance. Welcome to you all.

If you are not a part of the aforementioned groups, please don't leave. This sermon is meant to be overheard, even though it is directed at the graduating class.

Members of the graduating class of 1997 of Saint Thomas Choir School: I believe I have come to know some things about you just by watching you this year. Watching you sing or perform your acolyte duties, hearing what your choirmaster and your teachers and your headmaster and your clergy say about you, conversing with you myself, taking weekly meals at the school, all this has given me a picture of you that gives me confidence when I think of your entering the new frontier of high school.

I have thought of many things I would like to say to you, but I didn't think you would remember them. There is too much going on in your lives at this exciting time. So I'll try to keep this clear and simple, and mercifully short. I want you to remember five things. Five things you already know but must not forget. I'll give you four, and we'll save the fifth till the end.

Four things: (1) Please. (2) Thank you. (3) Smile. (4) A firm handshake and a clear look in the eye. I'll repeat them: Please. Thank you. Smile. A firm handshake and a clear look in the eye.

Let me elaborate just a little.

Please. When you want something, say please. Saying please means that you realize that what you are asking for may not be yours by right. That it is not yours to take for granted. When you say please, you acknowledge the position of the other person and his or her freedom to grant or decline your request. When you say please you respect his or her dignity. The acknowledgment and respect that is implied when we say please is one of the cornerstones of what we call civilization and is a basic Christian virtue. Saying please helps prevent civilization from becoming barbaric; it helps keep the peace between people; when individuals, groups and even nations say please, it helps prevent fighting and wars.

Thank you. This is very important. Please and thank you are like rock 'n' roll. They go together. There is a story in the Gospel about Jesus and ten lepers. All ten came to Jesus and said, Lord, please heal us. He healed them, all ten. But only one of the ten returned to Jesus praising and thanking God. Jesus remarked, Were not ten healed? Where are the other nine? The pleases outnumbered the thank-yous by a proportion of ten to one. I'm afraid that's the way it is with us, but with ladies and gentlemen, the ratio should be much better. Saying thank you acknowledges and praises the gift and the giver. Saying thank you increases the fund of goodwill in the world. Saying thank you warms up human relations and builds friendships because it shows appreciation. Saying thank you, cultivating the habit of gratitude, boosts the spirit of the one who says it. Saying thank you and counting your blessings keep you from being gloomy, keep you focused on the good, keep you from being a complainer. Saying thank you builds up happiness in you. Say thank you; cultivate the habit. Strive to have the thank-yous equal the pleases.

Smile. We were built by God to smile, not to frown. It takes far fewer muscles and less effort to smile than to frown. Of course, smiling is the outward and visible sign of a person who knows about please and thank you. Sometimes I get tired of the superficial smile, the put-on-a-happy-face routine—we all do. But smiling is important. It indicates what's inside you. Joy is a sure sign of the Holy Spirit. Christians have a reason to smile, because they know about Jesus Christ; they know God loves them; they know life and love are stronger than death and evil. They know that life, for all its sorrow and struggle, has a happy ending through the death and resurrection of Jesus. For the believer, life is not a fatal tragedy; it is a divine comedy. Sometimes, when you don't feel like smiling, but you smile anyway, you encourage the inward smile that goes with the outward gesture. That's a good habit, like courage. You look trouble in the eye, you remember that God is great and that good is stronger than evil, and you smile. It's an act of faith. So smile. You have all the reason in the world. God loves you.

A firm handshake and a clear look in the eye. When we have dealings with people, we often shake hands on it. It is a little ritual that goes back to the beginning of human life on this planet. It's what the Bible calls a covenant. You acknowledge the other person, you signify your goodwill, you present yourself with integrity. You don't have to like the other person, agree with him, or anything else. In fact, there will be many occasions when you have to have dealings with people you don't agree with, or don't like, or both. It is all the more important to give a firm handshake, not a dead, cold fish. It is all the more important to look the other person in the eye. Jesus said the eye is the light of the body. It is a window to the soul. It is very important to overcome shyness in this. My son was shy. I was very shy. Get over it. Give a firm grip and a clear look that say, "Hello, here I am, present and accounted for."

There they are: (1) Please. (2) Thank you. (3) Smile. (4) A firm handshake and a clear look in the eye. They are indispensable to getting along in this world. If you take nothing else from the Saint Thomas Choir School, take these things. And now one more. I didn't forget the fifth thing, the most important of all: (5) Trust God.

Trust God. You have been singing music to God's glory, you have been serving at the altar of Jesus Christ, you have been taught the graces of the Holy Spirit. These are all like swimming lessons, learning the strokes. Now take the plunge. Believe in God, trust God with all your heart. You find out that God is as good as his word. You can bet your life on it. I won't go on about this, because you have been with me Sunday by Sunday and you have already heard me at length. But trust God. Now one more time, all five: Please, thank you, smile, a firm handshake and a clear look in the eye, and above all and in all, trust God.

You are fine young men. Your parents are so proud of you. I am proud of you, we all are. We wish you all God's blessings and the very best of success in all you do. Remember us in your prayers, and come visit us from time to time, because it will be great to see you. You are part of our family. For heaven's sake, take good care of yourselves!

Good News: It's All True

YOUR CHRISTMAS THANK-YOU NOTES are late only after today. The Christmas cycle, following Saint Luke, runs from the birth of Jesus to his Presentation in the Temple by Mary and Joseph forty days later. This follows the requirements of the Law of Moses (Luke 2:22–40).

It is worth noting that the parents of Christ, who is the Word who makes all things, took the poor people's option for their sacrifice, two doves rather than a lamb.

Over the years I have preached on one feature or another of this deep, rich story: the Lord's submission to and fulfillment of the Law; Saint Luke's various levels of meaning with regard to the Temple (the building, new and old, Christ's Body); the image of our Lady Saint Mary, together with faithful Joseph, presenting the Son to the Father; and, of course, the shadow of sacrifice. But today we'll look briefly at the two old people in the story, the octogenarian widow and prophetess Anna and the elderly Simeon, who actually took up Jesus in his arms and blessed God.

Anna spoke of the baby to everyone who was looking for redemption in Jerusalem, and she must have known everyone. Simeon had been told by the Holy Ghost that he would not die before he had seen the Lord's Christ. And so the baby Jesus inspired Simeon to sing the hymn that is part of the Church's night prayers in Evensong and Compline, the Nunc Dimittis: "Lord, now lettest thou thy servant depart in peace according to thy word, for mine eyes have seen thy salvation…"

Now I have two stories for you, one old, one brand-new.

Four decades ago on a midweek winter evening, as part of a preparation for a vestry meeting in a Connecticut parish where I was briefly a curate, we read a shortened form of Evening Prayer. We were not in church, but just standing around a meeting table.

The week before, the parish had had a "Faith Alive" weekend, in which people from outside our parish came to bear witness to the presence and power of Jesus in their lives. It was simple, straight-forward testimony, like what the old Methodists did. Several of the vestry members had attended the weekend.

I noticed that one of these members—the warden who minded the church property—seemed silent yet moved. We got through the business of the vestry meeting, which took about an hour, and then were breaking up to go home for the night. Although young and the new curate, I was already fond of Dan and approached him to ask, "Are you okay?"

"Oh yes, Andy, I'm okay. Very okay. It's just that I finally get it after all these years in church." "Get what, Dan?" "Jesus. I'm right with that old man's hymn tonight. I can go home in peace. My eyes have really seen thy salvation. Good night, Andy."

I can't recall many details beyond this, except that Dan seemed a more happy, peaceful man after that night.

That's the old story; now the new one. While I was preparing this homily on Friday morning, the following email arrived from a man half a continent away who is a worker in another denomination.

"I am writing to thank you for a Christmas present that you do not know you gave me.

"I am a church music director and I like to listen to the webcasts... Because of the nature of my work, it is a rarity that I get to listen to them live. So it was a particular treat that on Christmas morning, after all our services were over at church and all our presents had been opened at home, I got to log on to the website and listen in to your service as it was happening.

"I was (not very reverently, I'm afraid) reclined on the couch while our four-year-old son was on the floor amid boxes and wrapping paper, playing with the spoils of the morning. He was listening politely to the opening part of the Mass and once or twice perked up at a particular piece of music. When the sermon began, it quickly became clear that he was still listening. He never stopped playing with his toys, but he was asking questions about what was being said... You preached about the three births in the prologue to John's gospel that morning. It was one of those sermons that gathered steam as it progressed and ended to the effect that Love Almighty had come to make his home with us—that that incarnational love was, in fact, our home. My son never looked up, and he never stopped fiddling with whatever he was playing with—but at the end of the sermon he said, *very* quietly, 'Is it true?'

"With a lump in my throat, I told him that yes, it was absolutely true. At that moment, of course, all the fuss and bother and worry and effort that can be loosely termed 'working at a church during the month of December' shrank to insignificance. That was my best present this year, and I wanted to thank you for your part in it."

A few years ago an old friend, a distinguished priest educator, came to town to take me out to lunch. He has experienced much of the world, its glories and its sorrows. He is clear, direct, firm and brave. I was waiting for him at our front desk. It was February. In he came, saying, "Hello, Andy, I have good news for you." He had recently retired, having completed an extraordinary career. "What's the good news?" I asked eagerly. "The good news," he said, "is that it is all true."

Made in the USA
Lexington, KY
19 October 2014